FC
Fatherland

*A British boy's struggle stranded in
wartime Germany and his return home*

by Paul Briscoe

Hitler Youth Membership book belonging to Paul, showing his stamped identity picture and signature

Published by: BARNY BOOKS
Hough on the Hill, Nr Grantham, Lincs NG34 2BB
Fax: 01400 251737

ISBN N°: 1 903172 22 5

Produced by TUCANNdesign&print
19 High Street, Heighington, Lincoln LN4 1RG
Tel & Fax: 01522 790009

After many talks to schools, Institutes of Further Education, Rotary and Round Table clubs, Women's Institutes and Historical Organisations mostly in Suffolk, this book has finally been written.

Much help and encouragement has come from my family. Without the invaluable help from Helen Acton many of my Germanic stumblings would never have reached the final version for the Printer.

I am also very grateful to Molly Burkett of Barny Books for her vision, enthusiasm and enouragement, also to Tom, Barrie and Ben of TUCANN*design&print* for their very skilled handling and final production of the book.

Very sincere thanks to you all,
Paul Briscoe, Summer 2002

Introduction

Reflections on my past and perhaps a way of reconciling my past with now.

In a hectic flight from London to Dusseldorf and a mad drive by hire-car along the Autobahn to Kassal we had arrived in Wolfhagen.

'Paul, you must come to Pam's wedding, a family wedding, bring your family as well'.

So here we were in Schloß Waldeck, high above the Edersee and its tranquil expanse, dotted with sailing boats and idle, small fishing punts drifting in the midsummer sun. The castle was built around the mid-1100s. I was turning my glass of 'Sekt' thoughtfully and looking over the ramparts towards the distant dam, so terribly breached in the spring of 1943 by the 'Dambusters'.

A German couple near us spoke to their children, telling them, while furtively pointing at us: 'Das sind Englander'. No malice or hidden meaning. Was I an 'Englander' or was I a 'Deutscher'? In 1943 I can remember wanting to take revenge on the Englander. Now I found myself thinking, 'Weren't we (the English) clever?' 'Where do I stand?' This question has posed itself over and over again and sill does, but now it is much easier to solve and I can laugh at myself.

So, soon after this, when we came to toast the Bride and Groom with this marvellous backdrop, I could respond to both 'Our English friends!' and 'Unsere deutschen Freunde!' Why do we have to fight a war to do this?

The main cast

My father: Reginald Robert Briscoe — 1899-1932 a Cumbrian
My mother: Norah Constance (née Davies) — 1899-1995 of Irish/Welsh descent
Myself: Christopher Paul — July 1930- born South London

German Foster Parents: Hildegard Wyrich
Seppl Weyrich
Their son: Christian Weyrich
Seppl'e mother: Oma Sauter
Seppl's step-father: Opa Sauter
Seppl's sister: Maria Schwinn and husband Willi Schwinn, architect

My wife: Monica Ruth Briscoe (née Larter) 1930-
Our daughter: Catherine Ruth 1960-
Our son: Robert John 1962-

The English Boy in Germany

I was born in July 1930 in Streatham which is in South London. My memories are of parks and shops and trams and of Beatrice, the rather deaf lady who looked after me while my mother was at work. I can't remember my father. He had died when I was two and mother had gone back to her job as a reporter for The Daily Mirror. She also did some freelance work for other papers and women's magazines. She told me a lot about my father. He had been a quiet man who loved tinkering with his car and looking after his terriers. My mother was completely different. She loved life. She liked parties and travelling. Her great friend, Molly, shared her interests. She was a tour guide and Mother started going with her when she went abroad. That was how the two of them first went to Germany. They loved it there. They stayed at a pension where Nazi Party officials also stayed and they were very friendly to the two English ladies. Molly and Mother were flattered by their attentions. They loved going about with them and being driven around in a black, open topped Mercedes with the Nazi flag on the bonnet and waving at the people who saluted them as they went past. Mother was very impressed with the German sense of nationalism and the sense of pride they had in their own country. She thought it was all so wonderful.

I was quite happy staying at home with Beatrice. I liked going off to the Rudolf Steiner Kindergarten each morning by taxi and I loved playing in the park with

England 1934 aged 4

Beatrice. She always spoiled me. Then Seppl came and stayed with us. Mother had met him on one of her visits to Germany and, when he had said that he wanted to come to England to improve his English, she had invited him to come and stay with us. I didn't like him from the start. He ordered me around and kept saying that he would make a man of me. I was pleased when he went back to Germany and Beatrice and I had long days on our own. But that wasn't to be for long.

Germany 1935

Mother had been doing more and more freelance work and Seppl had persuaded her to go to Germany. He convinced her that there were many stories to be found there and that the growth of the Third Reich was the most important event of the century. I didn't understand that but I did know that we were going off on a big adventure. I can remember the excitement with which we set off for Croydon Airport.

I sat close to Mother on the aeroplane. It didn't feel safe at all. It looked so flimsy and it made such a noise when the engines started up. I was frightened especially when we landed in Belgium before going on to Frankfurt. A strong wind was blowing and men ran along beside the plane when we touched down on the runway, throwing ropes over the wings and hanging on to them for dear life, trying to slow us down. We stopped right at the end of the runway. When we set off again, I needed to go to the toilet but, when I lifted the seat, I was looking down on the fields and houses a long, long way beneath us, so I decided not to bother and went and sat down beside Mother.

Frankfurt was bewildering. It was so different to Streatham. I held on to Mother tightly. It all seemed so busy and I couldn't understand what anyone was saying. Nobody had told me that they would be talking in a different language. Even if they had, I wouldn't have understood what a language was. We made our way to the railway station and got on to a train. It wasn't a bit like the trains back in London. This had slatted wooden seats and it was crowded with people,

Cowboy (Carnival) Lina, 2nd from left

noisy people who chattered and laughed and jostled and had lots and lots of belongings, chickens and rabbits in boxes, hampers and cardboard boxes tied with string. When the train started, people broke off pieces of bread from long loaves and ate them along with slices of strong smelling sausage or cheese and onion. A lady offered some to me but I sank back behind my mother and she said something to the lady in this strange language. People got off at every station and others got on but at last we drew into a bigger station, Miltenberg. This was where Seppl lived.

A tall stationmaster in a blue uniform with gold braid stood on the platform, shouting, "Miltenberg, alles aussteigen. End-station" (Miltenberg. All off. End of line). He blew his whistle and held up a long signal stick, red on one side and green on the other.

A taxi took us up into the town, a town that to my childish eyes looked wonderful. We drove along beside the river where barge upon barge was going up and down, then up to the main part of the town with glimpses of narrow, cobbled streets and alleys and rising above the town were the hills and the castle that looked as though it had been there since history began. We stopped at the Brauerei Keller where Tante Lina folded me to her ample bosom and, from then on, spoilt me silly all the time we stayed at this particular guest house. The arrangement suited Mother very well. She could leave me there safely and go out and meet her friends and get stories. It was a pattern that was set for the next two years. I can't remember how long we stayed in Miltenberg but, whenever I could escape from Aunt Lina's clutches, I would go out and play with the other children. The trouble was that I couldn't understand what they were talking about and they couldn't understand me. They thought I was odd and started to call me names. I didn't know what they meant but I knew they were bad, so I put my fists up ready to fight them every time they shouted after me. They thought that was great and started to call me Max Schmelling who was a famous German boxer at that time. I didn't like that either but that only made the boys shout it out louder. When Mother came home

7

I told her that the children kept saying that I was smelling. She laughed and explained who Max Schmelling was. I didn't mind being called after a boxer, especially a famous one.

Some of the bigger boys started trying to teach me German and calling me: 'Zamer Engländer'. They would make me repeat words over and over again until I got them right but, when I went back to the pension and told Aunt Lina what I had learned, she would cover her head with her pinafore and say that I was not to say those words again. It was all very bewildering to a four year old.

But we were soon on the move again. Mother had sent some stories back to London but she needed to get to the bigger towns where things were really happening. We went to Frankfurt first and stayed in a pension there. I expected Frankfurt to be like Streatham but it wasn't.. There were trams clanking their way along the roads and horse and carts carrying all manner of things and groups of Germans arguing and gesticulating until I was sure a fight was going to break out but it never did. Mother was really busy doing interviews and attending meetings, filing reports and researching material for articles and stories. Then, in the evenings, she would type them up. She always seemed to be busy and didn't have a lot of time to spend with me. She would ask other English guests to look after me and I met a lot of kind people who would take me out and buy me sweets. I began to pick up a few words of German but Mother and I spoke English and most of the other guests in the pensions where we stayed spoke English as well. Sometimes, when there wasn't anyone to look after me, Mother would take me to a kindergarten but it was generally only for a few days. Once when we were staying at the Pension Weber in Frankfurt, I went to the kindergarten for several weeks. I was excited when I was chosen to be one of the Ten Little Nigger Boys in the concert they were giving but I never actually got on to the stage. I was the reserve and had to wait at the back of the stage while the other children played their parts. Looking back, I always seemed to be the reserve. I was desperate to be included, to be the same as the other children but we never stayed anywhere long enough for that.

Mother was a happy go lucky person but her moods could change in an instant. One day, she took me to have my hair cut while we were staying in Frankfurt. My blonde curls came down to my shoulder. She sat and read a magazine while the barber cut my hair, German

Germany, 1939, showing acquisitions by Hitler up to the outbreak of World War II and Post World War II Germany

'Iron Curtain' ▬▬▬
(East & West Germany 1961-1989)

fashion, leaving my head shorn except for a small quiff on my forehead. My mother exploded when she saw me, bursting into tears and shouting at the barber until people gathered in the doorway to see what was happening. By the time we got back to the pension, she was her old happy self again.

Mother was always looking for newsworthy stories. As soon as we got settled in one place, we would have to move on, Frankfurt, Stuttgart, München.........

Mother was often short of money and we would have to buy food and eat it in our room rather than go to a restaurant. It took me a long time to understand why we had to do that. One day, I discovered that a lot of our belongings had disappeared and saw that she was no longer wearing her ring. When I asked her where it was, she didn't answer. But as soon as an envelope came from England, she went down to a shop and got it back. She had pawned it. For a while we would have the best room again and eat at the most expensive restaurants.

When we first went to a guest house, Mother would insist that we

Miltenberg Market Palce, the shop is on the left

had the best room. But it wouldn't be long before we had to move to a cheaper one and we would frequently finish up in the attic. Those attic rooms could be really cold in the winter and really hot in the summer. I can remember being very ill when we were in an attic in Stuttgart. Mother was desperate for money but she obviously didn't like leaving me. Then Seppl and his friend came to see us. He brought me some marzipan animals and he was very kind. The next day, an envelope came from England. Mother was so frantic to open it that she tore the envelope and the money it contained. She knelt on the floor and pieced the notes together again and we moved back to a more luxurious room.

From then on, I went and stayed with Seppl and his family when Mother took her stories back to London. She would pick me up when she returned and we would carry on wandering from pension to pen-

1936 Oma Sauter & Paul aged 6

sion and town to town. Miltenberg was the calm in my life, the place where I began to know people and have an identity of my own. I loved it there. There was everything that was magic to a small child, the castle with the hills towering above it, the wide river with its busy traffic, the narrow streets and old houses and, above all, the family which I came to look on as my own.

Seppl was now my foster father. Opa and Oma Sauter lived with us and so did Seppl's sister, Maria.

They always welcomed me. They owned a furniture shop in the main square and lived above the business. Their life was a mixture of family and business. Nothing was allowed to get in the way of the business. It was such a different life to the one I had with Mother. I had regular warming meals. My clothes were always washed and ironed and ready for me to wear each day. Slowly those clothes changed to those more suitable for a German child than the ones my Mother had bought for me in England. I wore lederhosen, leather shorts that would last a lifetime, colourful braces and stout boots with long woollen socks in the winter and short socks in the summer.

I went back to Miltenberg in July when I was six. It was going to be time for me to start school in September. Mother arranged that I would stay with Seppl and his family

Oma, Opa, 1936 a Danish friend and Paul

11

and go to the local school. At first she came to see me frequently and she always had plenty to tell us about her experiences and adventures. We never knew when she was coming. She would often blow in like the wind and be gone again before I had had a chance to tell her what I had been doing.

I started school in September. I still had difficulty with the language but my teacher, Herr Arnold, was very kind and helped me a lot and I was soon speaking as fluently as the boys and girls in the class. That was all I ever wanted, to be like the other children. Even though they accepted me and I joined in all their games, there was still a certain reservation. I was still called Der zame Engländer.

We only went to school in the mornings, starting at eight o'clock in the winter and half past seven in the summer. We had the afternoons free, free to play in the woods and in the snow in winter. We made our own skis and played ice hockey with old walking sticks and tin cans. It was paradise for a small boy without a care in the world, who had spent so much time shut in guest house rooms.

Things changed in my second year. Discipline became stricter. Our teacher Herr Göpfert was a local party official, a fully paid up member of the uniformed branch of the Nazi party, the S.A. - the Sturm Abteilung, (Storm Section). He was a small squat man who never smiled. He was vain and arrogant and strutted round in his uniform as if he was Hitler himself. He didn't like me. He used every opportunity to remind me that I was not German, I was English. He made me really want to forget my own country. I now spoke German all the time. I didn't want to speak English. I wanted to be like the other children. He would ask me the English for a certain word and I wouldn't be able to remember it. That was a good excuse for him to mock me. "What! You're an English boy and you don't know your own tongue."

He didn't think I was good at anything. We had to stop using the Roman script. Instead we used a stilted Germanic script. We had to practise writing it and mine was considered the best.

Herr Göpfert couldn't believe that I, an English boy, had done the best German writing.

I think we were all a bit frightened of him, I know I was. He was a strict disciplinarian with a warped sense of humour of which I was often the target. One day, April 1st, he sent me to the chemist to fetch a box of 'Know-it-all' and, when I returned without it, he made a great joke of me. He was also a sadist. He would call boys out to the front on the slimmest excuse and cane them, pulling out his cane which he kept on clips beneath his desk. The look on his face when he was inflicting pain was one of sheer pleasure.

We had greeted Herr Arnold with the words, "Grüss Gott," when he came into the classroom. Now, when the teacher came into the room, we would give the Nazi salute and say, "Heil Hitler, Herr Göpfert," and he would reply in the same way.

Our school was a Catholic school. About three quarters of the town were Catholic. There was also a Protestant Church and school and a Synagogue which we passed on our way to and from school.

We played the usual childish games but there were lots of Hitler Youth displays and national Folk Festivals, Maypole dancing and traditional singing and dancing as well as army rallies and march pasts. There were rowing festivals on the river, shooting galas and swimming races.

We used to love the drum and fanfare bands at the Hitler Youth rallies and looked forward to the day that we would be old enough to join in. It was all very patriotic.

Then there was the Church with all its saints' festivals. We would have processions and pilgrimages to holy places. The main pilgrimage each year was to Walldürn about fifteen miles away. There would be a band leading us and a choir. Then there would be members of the Church and the priest with men holding a canopy over him, followed by other men carrying figures of Christ and Mary and some of the saints. The men had to be strong because the figures were heavy. The congregation came behind the procession with, sometimes, another choir. Cripples and sick people would be carried or pushed in wheelchairs so that they could touch the relics and probably be cured. We set off very early in the morning and, when we reached Walldürn, we would have a service and go to the fair and then walk home again in our long line.

There were always big parades on Hitler's birthday in April. We would often have a military band and a march past of soldiers goose stepping eight abreast. We would run along beside them waving our Swastika flags and singing to the tune that the band was playing. There would be Hitler Youth units and large black staff cars with flags flying.

It was all very exciting to a small boy.

Germany was vibrant, but there were some things that even as a young child I didn't like. I couldn't choose my own friends. The family would forbid me to play with some of the boys. There was one boy who lived under the Castle walls and I was forbidden to have anything to do with him. I never knew the reason why. Perhaps he was Jewish. I was encouraged to be friends with children whose families were customers in the shop.

The thing that really frightened me was their celebration for St. Nikolaus on the 6th December. This was more important in Germany than Christmas day. It had become dark early and it was snowing. I had been told horrific stories about St. Nikolaus and his assistant Knecht Ruprecht. I knew they were coming and I felt apprehensive. I didn't know what to expect. There was a knock on the front door at five o'clock and Oma Sauter went downstairs to open it. There was a lot of stamping and groaning and clanging of chains. Up the stairs it came, very slowly.

"Wo is der Paul?" a voice demanded.

I was trembling as we waited in the living room. The benevolent figure of St. Nikolaus came in first. He looked larger than life in his red coat, carrying a staff and a faggot broom and a large, important looking book. He opened the book slowly.

"Now then," his voice boomed, "what do I see? You don't always eat up your soup or potatoes. You never wash behind your ears. Homework is badly done. You leave your belongings all over the place. Have you done any good things?"

Then he turned to Knecht Ruprecht who had been hiding behind him. What a dreadful sight he was! He was dressed all in black like a chimney sweep. He had a black face and menacing teeth with chains hanging round his neck which clanged as he moved.

"In den Sack!" he exclaimed and lunged at me.

I screamed as he caught hold of me and stuffed me into the big, black coal sack. I struggled to get out but I was held firmly. The sack was flung over his shoulder and he started to move towards the stairs.

"Bitte, bitte, lass mich rauss!" (Please let me out).

Then I heard the kindly voice of St. Nikolaus. "Ja, lass ihn rauss. Now will you work hard and be sensible and clean."

I would have promised the earth to get out of that dreadful sack. I was sobbing as I climbed out, but the torture hadn't finished. St Nikolaus demanded that I sing a Christmas song and then recite a poem. It was almost more than I could do, I was sobbing so uncontrollably. I managed to utter a few words somehow but it must have been obvious that I was almost at the end of my tether.

"Good," St. Nikolaus said, "I can see you mean well. Give him the Rute."

This was a small faggot broom hung with sweets, dried fruits and small toys.

I was too shocked to appreciate them. When I asked why this had happened. I was told it would do me good but it was an experience that gave me nightmares for a long time.

Christmas eve in contrast was a magical time. There were snow covered streets and the sound of horse drawn carts going over the cobbles and sleighs being drawn by horses past the snow laden Christmas tree in the square. The whole town seemed to turn out for High Mass. We, the Ministraten (communion servers) lined up with candles to lead everyone to the altar. The choir sang the Te Deum and the whole Church was filled with the sound of singing as so many voices joined in the hymns. Then home and, when the little bell summoned us, we all went into the best room where the Christchild had been and there, under the Christmas tree lit with real candles was the crib and the presents, small but beautiful, hand carved wooden toys, small books and home made biscuits. There were hugs and kisses and, at long last, a warm bed with a large copper hot water bottle.

The priest was an important man in town. He taught religion at school and yet there was very little love or religion about him. He was a tall, thin gaunt man who wore a black gown and steel spectacles and he always looked disgruntled. He was always on about sin, hellfire and brimstone. He would hit us across the knuckles with his sharp edged cane if we displeased him and we displeased him a lot. He rode a big, black bicycle which he mounted by standing on two pins that extended from the spindle of the back wheel. We had to greet him by saying, "Grüss Gott," the same as we did when we went into shops but that was changing. Shops started to put up notices saying that they greeted people by saying, "Heil Hitler," in their shop. Despite my feelings for the priest, I served at the altar in Church. I soon became more Catholic than the Catholics.

There was always plenty happening in Germany, always plenty to do. Only going to school in the mornings left us plenty of time to play and there were all kinds of adventures we could have in the countryside around Miltenberg. Nobody at home was very interested in my progress. It was always the business and the success of the shop. I was free to roam the woods and meadows. The Olympic Games had been held in Berlin in 1936. We had seen all about them on the newsreels at the film shows. From then on, athletics and sports became very important. Boys that were good at them were given a lot of encouragement. I wasn't one of them but there were plenty of other ways to occupy our time. Our games tended to follow the seasons. We built dens and tree houses in the summer. In Autumn we collected mushrooms and berries, wild strawberries and bilberries and wild fruits and leaves for herbal teas. In winter when the snows came we made skis from old barrels or tobogganed down the slopes and then, when the snow melted, we dammed the streams or waded in the flooded fields.

A group of us were playing by the river when we heard this buzzing and it grew louder. Then we saw this long, dark shape in the sky. It was our first sight of the Zepellin. We could see people behind the windows looking down at us. We waved at them and they waved back. We could see the tail fins and the sunlight reflecting on its silvery white expanse. It went over us and disappeared downstream at about the speed of a slow car. Fishing was forgotten and I rushed home to tell the family what I had seen. Seppl told me proudly that this was the future transport in the sky and that it was a German invention. Everything of merit seemed to be German.

When I was lucky, I would go out in the afternoons with Seppl to deliver goods in our very ancient Citroen delivery car. It was always fun to pass fields and farms where you would see a cow and a horse in harness together pulling a plough or a big laden wagon. At harvest time carts would come to a large area under Miltenberg's main bridge where a huge threshing machine driven by a steam engine would be threshing well into the night under floodlights.

Later would come the time of the apple harvest when smaller carts came into a large pub near us that had a cider press.

One winter was particularly cold and the River Main froze over. The ice was so strong that traffic drove over it.

I never had a special friend. At first I played with any group that would have me but I soon became accepted and joined in with any adventure that was going. I first noticed that one or two of the boys with whom we played had disappeared. They didn't tell us they were leaving. They simply weren't there one day and their houses were empty. I didn't think too much about it until one boy who was going to meet me didn't arrive at our meeting place. I asked about him when I got home and Oma said that he had probably gone abroad like the others and Seppl added that he was a Jew. It didn't mean anything to me. It was just another fact that I didn't understand.

A very big event in 1937 was the 700th anniversary of the award of town status to Miltenberg in 1237. The celebrations went on from the 21st August to 30th finishing with a massive firework display. The town was full of colour with German flags hanging from many windows.Our most exciting day was a re-enactment of the storming and capture of the town by the Swedish King Gustav Adolf in 1631. In the pageant on Sunday 22nd August we had mock battles with the smell of burning and gunpowder everywhere. The clatter of horses and wagons galloping through the cobbled streets was mixed with screams of wounded Germans and Swedish mercenaries. We loved it and watched the mock battles from the back garden, a real war for us to watch without coming to any harm!

In May of 1938, we moved into a new class which was in an annex of the school half way up the hill with views from all the windows looking out over the hills and downstream of the river. Our path to school each day took us up flights of stone steps, along paths under the old town wall and through a neglected, dark cemetery. There were heavy gravestones there with strange writing which we couldn't decipher. The letters were different to the ones we used in school. We found out later that this was the old Jewish cemetery. There was an old tower in the corner that was called The Witches' Tower. It was where they had burned the witches in the middle ages. I hated walking past it and tried to avoid it if I could but it didn't bother the other boys. I tried not to let them see my feelings. They would have thought I was soft. We had begun to hear the words Jew and Jewish although we didn't really know what they meant except that they followed a different religion to ourselves.

We didn't know much about what was going on in the world outside the town. We only had the local paper at home, but we heard

more and more about what was happening elsewhere from radio programmes and films that we saw each Saturday at the children's film
shows, but as they didn't concern us, they were soon forgotten.

We heard that our Austrian brothers had come home to the German Fatherland. As they spoke the same language and had the same
religion, we could never understand why they had been apart from
us. There didn't seem to be anything wrong with the arrangement.
Anyway, I had other things to think about. My cousin Robin came to
stay with us when his mother went into hospital for an operation. He
was five years older than me and a real British public school boy but
the difference in age didn't seem to matter. I enjoyed showing him
around but the visit was shortlived. A telegram summoned him home
because his mother had died. It had been great having someone of my
own even if it was only for a couple of weeks. I was seeing less and less

1938 Seppl, Robin, my cousin and myself by the River Main

of my mother. It seemed that she was so busy. I didn't worry. I was
happy.

Our lessons began to change. We were taught more and more about
the superiority of the Germans and what was wrong with other nations. The way that Britain had colonised other countries was wrong
although I never knew quite why. There was criticism of the Jews and

18

we had text books showing Jewish men with big noses and evil smiles. The radio, newspapers and filmreels at the cinema carried similar messages.

But there were lots of good things happening. The rallies were getting bigger and the giant Mayday rallies were real spectacles. The biggest May tree we had ever seen went up in the main square. The whole town was decorated with German flags strung across the narrow streets. An army unit marched past and saluted the local Gauleiter (head of the local Nazi party). They were lead by the Hitler Youth drum and fanfare band. Then came other groups taking over an hour to march past. Then members of the B.D.M. (the girls' branch of the Hitler Youth) gave a demonstration of Maypole dancing. This was followed by folk dancing and band festivals. There was always something happening. I envied the boys in the Hitler Youth and couldn't wait to be old enough to join in with all their activities.

Things were happening with the family. Maria and Willy were married and we all went to Frankfurt for the ceremony. They did not marry in the church but in the Registry Office and took their vows over a copy of Mein Kampf rather than the Bible.

It was about this time that Seppl brought Hildegard home, the girl that he was to marry the following summer. I grew very fond of Hildegard. She became an important part of my life.

A film crew arrived in the square. They were making a film about Germany called Spiel in Sommerwind, (Play in the Summer's Wind) and they were looking for two typically German children to be in it. I was chosen to be the boy and I did look German with my blue eyes and blonde hair and dressed in Lederhosen, carved horn braces and traditional Bavarian socks. An Aryan girl, with her blonde plaits and dirndl skirt had also been chosen and we had to chase each other round the fountain. I had to catch her and steal a kiss. I never thought it odd, that I, an English boy, was playing the part of a German. I was too interested in my payment, five marks and a large bar of chocolate.

One of the little shops opposite ours was a haberdashers run by an elderly Jewish lady called Mira. She was small and dark and friendly. I was in bed on the night of November 8th when I was woken up by a lot of shouting. I went across to the window to see what was happening. People with torches on long poles were marching up the street from the river towards the Marktplatz. There was a crowd following them. They stopped outside Mira's shop and started throwing stones at her windows and shouting. I opened the window to hear what they were calling out.

"Rauss dü Judin! Rauss du Schwein!" (Out you Jew! Out you pig!)

The long poles were used to break the upstairs windows but nothing happened and the crowd started shouting louder. Then one of the top windows opened and Mira looked out, a terrified old woman in a nightshirt. "Was ist das?" she called out. "Warum all das?" (what is all this? What is up?)

The shouting grew louder still but there was laughter and mocking in their voices. They wanted her out. The shouting and noise went on and on and eventually Mira came downstairs and opened the door. Now the crowd took up a new call, "Rauss, rauss, rauss." They had smashed the shop window by this time and rolls of cloth, ribbons and all manner of things were being tossed about with a lot of mocking laughter. And then Mira tried to get away and started to run down the street and the crowd ran after her,. shouting and goading her, poking her with their long poles. I can picture her now, a little old lady struggling to escape from their taunts.

I never knew what happened to her. When I asked about her at home, my questions were ignored or I was told that the Jews deserved this treatment. They controlled the world's money. Nobody would answer my questions. When I went to school the next day, I walked through spoilt ribbons and soiled reels of cotton and other goods. They were there for a long time. Nobody bothered to clear them up.

We went to school as usual the next day but we were told that we were to take part in a rally to show how strongly we supported the Führer. We lined up and were marched down to the synagogue which was opposite our old infant school. Local brownshirts and party activists were out in force, lining either side of the road. The older secondary school boys were already there in their Hitler Youth uniforms. They were full of aggression and bravado.

"Break it up. Get the Jews out," was shouted and everyone took up the call until it became a threatening crescendo of sound.

Some men started to break down the doors and a lot of the older boys rushed to help them. Nobody tried to stop them. The teachers stood at the side of the road and watched with smiles on their faces. Then we were all filing, then rushing into the building. I stood and looked round me. I had often wondered what it was like inside the synagogue, now I could see for myself and I felt awed. It wasn't like our Catholic Church but it still held an air of sanctity and peace, but only for a few seconds. The older boys had gone to the balcony and started throwing hymn books at us and we started to throw them back, hesitatingly at first. Then, when we saw that nobody was going to stop us, we gave as good as we got. Kneelers followed the books. Then we got on to the balcony and started throwing chairs and benches at the central chandelier until it crashed to the ground shattering into pieces amongst the debris. We ventured into the holy part where scrolls and precious items were kept. We dressed up in the vestments and pretended to be priests. None of the adults tried to stop us, in fact they seemed to approve of what we were doing, yet in our heart of hearts we knew it was wrong. I know I did.

Then the Rabbi came running in and started to plead with us to save his Church. We didn't take any notice. We started to mock him and throw books at him. We drove him out of his Church. The mob outside joined in the mocking and shouting. They started to throw whatever they could find at him until he was bleeding and shouting for mercy.

I can remember standing there and looking at the mob, recognising so many devout people that would attend the service in the Catholic Church the following Sunday.

Most of the Jews simply disappeared. I don't know what happened to them. Nobody gave them a thought. When Seppl came home one day, he said that he had seen some men working on the road. He supposed they were the Jews. We never thought there was anything wrong in this. I never heard anyone criticizing the way the Jews were being treated. Nobody expressed any sympathy for them. The people with whom I was living were reasoned and basically decent people but they were caught up in the thinking of the day. Neighbours and customers were no longer part of their world if they were Jewish. Now the Jews had to wear a yellow star of David, with the word Jude written in the middle. They were marked out and considered sub human. They were hounded and ridiculed.

There was always this suggestion that Jews were bad and Germans were good. Our lessons began to change, our text books at school showed caricatures of Jews as the villains. The questions in our maths books would suggest this. Herr Goldschmitt charges so much for a pair of slippers. Herr Schmidt charges a lesser amount. How much more profit does Herr Goldschmitt make than the German shop keeper?

Notices appeared telling us to be careful of enemies of the Third Reich and there would be a Jewish man depicted as the enemy.

We were taught more and more about the superiority of the Germans and what was wrong with other nations. The way that Britain had colonised other countries was wrong. There was criticism of the Jews and we had text books showing Jewish men always with money bags. The radio, newspapers and films at the cinema carried similar messages. One such film was set in South Africa and showed blacks herded into camps by the British and Boers. Soldiers would herd women and children into compounds and shoot them down. Another scene showed black women tied to the front of a British train trying to force its way through Boer lines hoping that the enemy wouldn't dare shoot at the women. The stories were always portraying fat mostly ugly Jews smoking fat cigars and eating too much. One SS Stürmer magazine I saw showed a whole line of black American negroes hanging after a mass execution in America.

We heard that there had been an attack on a German attache in Paris by a Jew. Dr Goebbels was our Minister of Propaganda and he made the most of this. We saw him on a newsreel on Saturday mornings telling us that the Jews must be controlled. It seemed the Jews held all the money markets of the world. I didn't understand what it all meant but I realised that Jews were bad.

I didn't know anything about hate. Baiting the Jews became part of our lives, a bit of fun for us children. I never had any feeling of guilt.

1939 was to be a big year for me. I was taking my first Communion at Easter and, in the summer, I was going back to England with my mother. I was excited about the first event but not sure about the second. I didn't want to leave Germany, not then. Too many exciting things were happening. In February and March our German troops marched into the fertile area surrounding most of Czechoslovakia and saved it from attack by hostile forces. The Böhmen and Mähren (Bohemia & Moravia) Protectorate was created. We were encouraged in Geography lessons to buy a set of stamps that marked the occasion.

First Communion with Aunt Lina in 1939

They cost all my pocket money but I was proud to have them. But this and all the other events were overshadowed by the preparations for our big day at Easter, our first Communion. We had a lot of special lessons to prepare us, most of them were dull and went over my head. My overwhelming impression of the whole course was the issue of sin and how we needed to rid ourselves of this terrible burden. We made lists of our sins and had guidance on minor, major and deadly sins. We searched our minds as to how many apples we had stolen from the orchard and what naughty pictures we had seen or how hard we had punched or hit others. Then it was time for our main confession. This was held in a forbidding looking cubicle with a curtain hiding the priest taking the confession. From behind the curtain a sensorious voice would interject asking us exact details of our sins.

When it was all over and all my life's misdeeds had been laid bare I almost fell out of the cubicle. I was drained but felt contrite as I said many hail Marys and Our Fathers to help me get clean.

Stepping up to the altar on my first Communion Day, I believed with all my heart as I took the host from the priest with a feeling of utter devotion and purity. I have never in all my life recaptured that absolute and pure moment.

Then came the fun side of the celebration and I was the centre of it all. I had the first helpings from a large dish of salads, meat and cheese, all arranged in the shape of a swan. My mother had joined us for the day. It was a really happy day but soon my mother had to leave. She was having to cover story after story that was unfolding in Munich, London, all over Europe. So much diplomatic activity was taking place but it didn't really concern me or the family except how it all might affect their business.

Mother returned to England for the last time in May and made arrangements to return in July near my ninth birthday when I would go back with her to England.

We were going home.

Prime Minister Chamberlain travelled back and forth to Berlin, having every faith in 'Peace in our time.' July came. There was no word from Mother. August came. Customs and border posts were carefully watched. There was still no word from my mother. I didn't mind. It was school holidays and I was happy. It turned out that she had been unable to get a visa to come out to Germany to fetch me. A Dutch friend was returning to Holland before it was too late. He promised to try and contact me and get me back to mother but we never heard from him. Then it was the first of September. Hitler declared war on Poland over the issue of a free corridor to link East Prussia with the Fatherland. Because England had this non aggression pact with Poland, she declared war on Germany on 3rd of September. It was the start of the Second World War.

They kept asking questions. Was I Aryan or perhaps I was Jew?

"Nonsense," my German family answered, "he is a Catholic. He has taken his first Communion."

"Good. Show us his papers."

That was the problem. I had no papers. Mother had taken them back to London with her.

There were more questions. Where was his birth certificate? Where were his immunisation and vaccination papers? I didn't think any of it was important. All I wanted was to get out and play with my friends. The days weren't long enough to worry about pieces of paper. But then I saw that the family were getting worried. I could hear them talking about these certificates and they would change the subject when I went into the room. Perhaps this was serious after all. Then I was questioned at school and always there was the question: Was I a Jew? I began to get worried.

A party official came to the shop and asked for my papers. If they didn't have them, we would have to get them.

"But his mother is in London and we are at war with England."

That was not their concern. Either we presented my papers or I would be sent to a camp for aliens. Hildegard came up with the answer. She and Seppl had married that summer so technically she was my foster mother. They would adopt me. That was fine but how would they be able to do that without my papers. One of the customers suggested that perhaps the Red Cross in Switzerland would be able to help and they did. They managed to contact my mother and she sent my papers to them and, after a delay of several weeks, they arrived with my new family. I was then formally adopted. It all took a long time but by the spring of 1940, everything was settled. I was officially German. I was issued with a ration card and I was entitled to join the Jungvolk, the under 14 section of the Hitler Youth.

If you wanted to take part in sports and activities, you had to belong to this and I wanted to take part more than anything else in the world. My baptismal certificate had been the major reason for my acceptance. A Catholic could not be a Jew. I can't explain how I felt when I knew everything was settled. It was more than pride. I was like the other boys now. I could become a young fighter and help in winning the war against the Jews and the Capitalists and the World Bankers. I was going to fight for my new country and for the Führer.

I was the proudest boy alive when I dressed in my uniform, black shorts and black top with a brown shirt and scarf and a leather knot to fasten the scarf tightly round my neck. I was issued with an achievement book to enter all the tests I passed. As a new member of the Jungvolk, I was known as a Pimpf. When I passed my Pimpfen Probe (test), I became a full member of the Jungvolk and was allowed to

carry a Fahrten Messer. This was a dagger, similar to a bayonet with a swastika marked on the handle which fitted on to your belt. I had to run 60 metres in 12 seconds, throw a ball 26 metres and long jump 2.75 metres to pass my test. I had to know the oath of the Jungvolk and the words of the Horst-Wessel song and the Hitler Youth Flag song.

It was all fun. We never thought of indoctrination but looking back now, I can see how gradually Nazi ideas were introduced until, in the regulations for the Hitler Youth Silver Award in the section called 'View of the

HJ (Jungvolk) Record Book photo

World', members were asked to give a racial political act by the State and explain its significance. Another question was; 'Our Fatherland can demand of us that, if necessary, we are willing to fight and give our life for our people. Why?"

This all went over my head. I was only interested in being the same as the other boys and having fun.

Being at war didn't make any difference to us at first except that I had to help in the business. Most of the able bodied men had joined the forces. In the first days, there had been queues of men waiting to sign up. Seppl had been one of the first. He had joined the army before war had been declared. So had Maria's husband, Willy Schwinn. I had a lot of respect for him. He was straight and honest and always had time to explain things to me. Maria had shut up her house and come back to live with the family so, when Willie came home on leave, he would come to the shop. He didn't come home often but Seppl was always managing to get extra leave and he never came home empty handed.

Hildegard my foster mother

After the first few weeks, things settled down much as before. It was a glorious autumn and there was plenty of time for us to play although most of our games were war ones. We saw newsreels of our glorious troops fighting for the Fatherland every Saturday morning. We heard about their advances on the radio. Opa would turn the wireless up so that he could hear every word. There was a lot of military music. Aeroplanes flew overhead. We would stand and watch them and feel proud of the black crosses marked on their wings. Most of the young men wore military uniforms.

But this was all in the background. We had more time on our own and with the men away at war and the women busy running their husbands' businesses, there was nobody to keep us in order and we started to run wild. We would knock on people's doors and run away, throw stones at their windows and, if we thought they were Jewish, we would really go to town.

One day we found a slatted fence behind the castle wall and we started to break it up to use the wood for swords. A shriek from a lady when she saw what we were doing sent us running, but I was the last and with my mop of blonde hair, I was easily recognisable She shouted out for me to go to her. She took me into her house on the side of the town wall and told me to stay there while she phoned the police. A policeman soon came, a small disgruntled man with a handgun on his belt. He marched me off to the police station where he wanted to know which other boys were involved. I didn't tell him. I was marched down to the cells and the large wooden door was shut and locked behind the weeping criminal. I was left there for two or three hours and then I was marched home where the family were told to deal with me, and they did. They were all so involved with the business that they really did not have the time to know what I was getting up to but I was much more careful after that incident.

The Hitler Youth was different. The leaders seemed to know everything about us and discipline was strict and unquestioned. If we missed a meeting because of homework or having to do something at home, then our leader would be round to see our teacher or parents and there would be guarded threats about what would happen if we missed another meeting. Meetings were the priorities in our lives. As the war continued so they became more and more frequent. The best activities were always on Sunday mornings when we should have been going to Church. The priest spoke to the leaders but he had the same answer as our parents. Nothing had to stand in the way of our activities. So instead of going to Church, we went skiing or camping or rowing. It was fun and very important to us, more important than Church or our families. We were told how we were expected to behave. We were expected to look and listen to people in the town and if we heard anyone criticising the Führer or the Fatherland, then we were to report it straight away to our leaders. I had no intention of telling anyone what my family discussed in the home, but some of the boys did. They reported their own parents.

There was a lot of talk at home about what was happening in the War. Every broadcast finished with 'Heil Hitler.'. He was like a God to a lot of Germans at that time. There was talk on the wireless about our glorious troops and their victories. There were letters from Seppl and Willie which were read over and over again. We saw films of our conquering heroes on the newsreels each Saturday and their victories were discussed in school. Much was made of the capitulation of Paris and I felt so proud watching the film of our troops marching down the Champs Elysee in Paris with the Arc de Triomphe behind them. I couldn't wait to grow up and be one of them.

It was soon after this that Willie came home on leave. He was an architect in peace time and he had been given the job of designing the gun emplacement to go on top of the Eiffel Tower, 985 feet above the ground. I felt so proud of him and the job he had been given. I studied every drawing he made, watched him sketch every section, every elevation. I determined that one day I would be an architect like him. I felt superior walking down the road beside him in his smart uniform but Maria his wife found fault with him and grumbled. Seppl often came home on leave at that time and he always brought things he had managed to pick up, bottles of wine or something for the business. Maria thought her husband should do the same. Willie brought nothing. He was straight and honest and I respected him for it. It was a different matter after the war. Willie returned to Miltenberg as district architect, responsible for rebuilding the town, while Seppl, who had deserted from the German army and joined Tito's troops in Yugoslavia, was still trying to make his way home.

Then Germany invaded Russia. That was the first time I heard anyone in the family criticise Hitler. They quoted from Mein Kampf in which Hitler had said that no war should ever be fought on two fronts and we were fighting on three because we had gone to the aid of our Italian allies and were fighting in North Africa as well. Our troops had been poised at the Channel ports ready to invade England, why then had Hitler turned his attention to Russia? I sat and listened to what was being said. We only ever talked like this at home. There were plenty of people in the streets who were only too happy to report people that criticised the Führer to the party leaders.

At first we saw the invasion of Russia as another Blitzkrieg, (lightning war) and the newsreels encouraged us to think that way, but it was a turning point.. The war in Russia dragged on. The plan had been for the Germans to take Moscow before the winter set in but there had been problems from the beginning. A lot of our crack troops had been diverted to help Mussolini's troops in North Africa and the invasion of Russia had been delayed. The Germans had not expected the ferocity of the Russians or their tactics. We knew nothing of this. We believed all the stories we were being told and took them in with a patriotic fervour but hardships and shortages started to become apparent. A black market started to flourish. Laws were tightened. We were forbidden to listen to foreign radio programmes. Although we were at war with England, people liked to listen to the King's speech on Christmas day. There was an attempt to belittle him by making fun of his stammer. Lord Haw Haw often referred to it. People also liked to listen to London Calling but now, it was more than we dared to do. People who were caught breaking these and other laws simply disappeared. We didn't see them again. Notices also appeared. One that was pasted up everywhere was of a listening figure beneath which the message appeared, 'Der Feind hört mit', (The enemy is listening).

The Volks Sturm was created which was like the British Home guard. Propaganda strengthened but, at home, the family were beginning to question what was happening. I felt loyal to the Hitler Youth. After all, we were the future of The Third Reich. Our leaders were always telling us this but I was listening to the discussions at home and I started to have doubts.

SS Lifeguard review in 1939/40 by Hitler

It was about this time that I received the last letter from my mother. It was the fifth I had from her. They were very formal. She was only allowed to write twenty five words on a pre-printed Red Cross form. I could write twenty-five words back to her on the reverse side. It was all impersonal but now my links with England were finally broken. I didn't mind. I had plenty of other things to think about.

I was never very good at school but somebody must have seen something in me because I was offered a place at the Karl Ernst Gymnasium in Amorbach, some eleven miles south of Miltenberg. It was in an estate village with a large palace and park belonging to the Duke of Leiningen. He owned all the land and the huge forests that swept down to the banks of the River Neckar and Heidelberg. There was a monastery in the village and most of the teachers had been monks but they had all been called up so we were taught by nuns and secular teachers. I wasn't any better at this school than I had been at the primary one. The problem was that two of the main subjects were English and Latin and I wasn't any good at either of them. The English teacher used to say, "I can't understand it. You are English and you can't speak your own language." What she didn't understand was that I didn't want to speak it. I wanted people to forget that I had ever been English. I wanted to be part of this wonderful, victorious country.

There were good sides to the school though. We went by steam train each day through some of the most beautiful countryside - flower speckled meadows, cornfields, apple and cherry orchards, over streams and beside huge forests. There were many level crossings and we would lean out of the windows and shout at the girls cycling to school and wave at the bullock carts with their swaying loads of hay or fodder beet. Later on, in 1943, we would often be forced off the train and have to run down the embankment and shelter beneath the trees as the allied bombers flew in aiming to bomb the engines and damage the railway lines. There were many times that we were late home because the locomotive had been damaged and could only crawl back to Miltenberg. Once or twice we never got to school at all because the railway line had been bombed. I can't ever remember feeling frightened. It was all part of the excitement.

Late in 1941, a secondary school had been opened in Miltenberg and, at the end of 1943, we were transferred to it. There were no more exciting train journeys, we had to walk to the other side of the town instead.

It was about this time that the family decided I should learn how to play the piano. This would solve two problems. I had too much spare time and they had a piano in the living room. It was not successful. The piano was out of tune and it was a useful place on which to stack curtain material. Miss Heidel's idea of teaching the piano was as a mathematical exercise while holding two exercise books under my armpits to improve my posture. Her lessons were controlled by the ruler and the metronome. Any wrong timing or note was rewarded with a hit across my knuckles with her ruler. As the piano was also in the living room which doubled as the office and contained the only phone in the house, my playing was often curtailed by having the piano lid banged down on my fumbling fingers when someone needed to answer the phone.

Attitudes had begun to change at the end of 1941. We still heard all about our glorious victories but some of our soldiers were returning and they weren't always telling us the same things that we were seeing on the newsreels. The older people began to question but only in the privacy of their own homes.

I had wondered about what had happened to some of the boys with whom I used to play, especially the Jewish ones. Now one of the family would casually mention one of the families that used to be our neighbours. They always presumed that they had gone to live in Switzerland or America with their relations but one day, Seppl came home on leave and said that he had seen a party of Jewish men from the town repairing the roads.

Then on December the 7th, 1942, the Japanese bombed Pearl Harbour and we had a new ally, Japan. There were films telling us about the glorious Japanese troops. It was only at home that the family mentioned that it had also brought the Americans into the war as well - against us.

Wounded and crippled men were returning from the eastern front. Some of them had had limbs amputated because of frost bite. We were ordered to salute these heroes when we passed them in the streets. The Hitler Youth had to help with collecting days. There were more and more of these, collecting days for Winterhilfe, (winter help), collecting warm clothes and blankets for displaced German subjects returning from German settlements in the east. We were urged to save electricity for the Führer and we started having Eintopf Sundays where families would have one pot stews. It was the same in pubs and restaurants. The waiters would cut coupons from our ration books if we ate there.

Then, on 31st of January, 1943, our victorious troops surrendered at Stalingrad. It was difficult for us to take in because there was still news of our victories.

Air raids had become part of our lives. At first they had added to the excitement and we would watch the green flashes in the darkness towards the industrial north west and hear the echoes of our guns firing at them. Then the threat came nearer and the warning sirens screamed out their message. Most of the houses had cellars where people stored potatoes and coal and that sort of thing. Now they were converted to shelters. Bunk beds were taken down there and carpet laid on the floor. As soon as the siren went, we would file down into the nearest shelter. It became a way of life.

We would often watch enemy bombers flying overhead on their way to bomb a target further on and we would cheer our fighters as they went up to challenge them. We would cheer like mad when one of them seemed to get the better of the enemy plane when a dogfight ensued.

One summer afternoon, we were swimming in the River Main when two American bombers flew low over our heads. They were flying so low that they barely missed the treetops. They were well below the surrounding mountains. The first plane flashed by. It was so close that I could see the gold watch on the Negro rear gunner's wrist. I could even see the expression on his face. He was firing his gun at anything and everything.

We dived and swam for the bank under water. Tracer bullets were hitting the water. We clambered up the bank and took shelter under a haycart. We watched as the other bomber made its run along the valley. This one fired at a field on the other side of us where women and children were lifting potatoes. The women started screaming. Picking up their children, they ran for cover. A child was shot out of its mother's arms and the woman just stood there screaming. Then the plane banked and came in again. This time it seemed to be following one woman who was running for dear life. Then she fell. She had been shot dead. We stood up. We all did and we stared. The whole scene left us numb. Normal feelings were blanked out.

Guest workers were being moved into town and they were billeted in empty buildings. They came from countries to the east of Germany and few of them could speak German. Most of them in Miltenberg were Slavs. I think we knew that they were not being treated well but it didn't seem to be any concern of ours. After all, we had been brought up to believe that they were an inferior race to ourselves so their treatment seemed acceptable. They worked on the land or in factories but, later on, they helped the troops, carrying ammunition for the guns or digging trenches, that sort of thing. Hitler Youth cadets helped as well, manning the telephones or whatever was required.

All able bodied men were in the forces. Even the wounded were called back for certain duties. We were taught mainly by retired teachers who had returned to help or by sixth formers. They had to spend most of the time trying to keep order because the classes were huge, over a hundred to a class. More often than not, once they had achieved some semblance of order, the siren would go and we would all troop down to the shelters. Refugees were flooding into the town, escaping from their homes in front of the fleeing German troops. They brought hardly anything with them. There seemed to be more refugees than inhabitants and they were resented. Although they were considered German subjects, few of the children spoke the language which made our lessons even more disastrous.

Everything was short. All our supplies were needed for our gallant troops. I woke up with toothache one day, but the dentist told Hildegard that he couldn't fill my tooth unless she produced some silver, jewellery or a coin, that he could melt down and use for the filling. The family found enough and I took it along in a bag. The assistant melted it down in a crucible, cleared off the dross and my tooth was filled.

The Hitler Youth now had to help with the harvest. We assembled at the railway station carrying rucksacks with our bedding, spare clothes and mess tins. We were to gather in the hops. When the train reached the station, we clambered out and lined up behind the Hitler Youth flag. Then we marched to the farm singing patriotic songs with great gusto. Food was cooked in an army mobile boiler and we had to collect wood for the fire. It was fun out in the fields. We would sit on boxes and pull the hops from the fallen plants singing songs and telling each other stories. We put the hops in wickerbaskets and they were taken off to be dried. Then it was supper and songs round the camp fire, then sleep if we weren't interrupted by the rats or the snorers. The bugler was the worst blasting out so early in the morning when all we wanted to do was sleep. We got our own back though. We filled the snorers' mouths with toothpaste and poured ink into the bugle with soaked bread on top of it to keep it in.

We also helped with the potato and hay harvests but they were more local and we slept at home. We were paid but we all donated our pay to the German Red Cross, voluntarily of course!

Allied aeroplanes flying overhead were now a part of our daily life. They started to confuse the radar system by dropping strips of silver paper. One of our jobs in the Hitler Youth was to pick this up and take it to our leader but there was so much of it that we soon gave up. Then another menace appeared, - landmines. Sometimes we would be asleep in our own beds when the siren hadn't gone and there would be a huge explosion. We would be thrown on to the floor. A landmine had come down by parachute and landed a few streets away. They could have been dropped miles away and the parachutes would have carried them to the target. Sometimes they would destroy a whole street.

Sometimes, at night, we would hear distant rumbling, then the sky would light up and we knew a raid was taking place a long way away.

One bomb dropped at the edge of the town but failed to go off. We were forbidden to go near it and the whole area was cordoned off. We decided to dodge the police and get a look at this bomb. We could see where the crater was but we couldn't see the bomb. Then we heard this banging and clanging coming from that direction and we saw the police running towards it. They came back towing a boy behind them. We soon found out what he had done. He had taken a lump hammer and a chisel to the timing mechanism to get a souvenir of the bomb.

An allied plane crashed just beyond the town and we got there first. It was a New Zealand plane and only one of the crew survived. He had landed in a haystack. Most of the others were caught up in the trees. We descended on them like locusts. Somehow we didn't think of them as people. We took them down and emptied their pockets. We took their boots and cut up the parachutes. We even cut up the tyres. They were used for soling shoes. We took anything and everything that could be moved and got it hidden before the police arrived. I wonder now how we could have behaved in such a way. We showed the dead airmen no reverence. But we were children of the war. We had different values. The airmen were given a military funeral by the Volkssturm a few days later so they did get some respect.

Everything was in short supply but we still had goods in the shop, things that people needed, furniture, prams, lino, curtains. We had real currency. The goods were more valuable than money. It was now my turn to do something useful, not for the Führer but for the family. I would get up early, about four o'clock, and set off with a rucksack on my back. I made for the hills behind the castle through the dense, dark woods. I often saw wild animals, deer and wild boar which would give me a wide berth but there was one day I had to run for my life. I disturbed a family of young boar that were grazing away from their mother. Their squeals alerted her and she came at me at full speed. I had been warned about the boar often enough and I knew I had to get behind a tree which I managed to do but only just in time.

There was another occasion I had the fright of my life. It was still dark and I was making my way through the woods when something fell across my shoulders. I didn't know who was trying to catch me and I didn't wait to see. I turned and ran. Oma was surprised to see me back so early and wanted to know why I had a rope round my shoulders. I never did work out how it had fallen on me.

Generally my journeys into the hills were calm and peaceful. I came out of the forests on to the fertile fields and small hamlets of the Odenwald. Here, I would barter for food. I had my favourite places. There was one farm where I was always invited for breakfast and I would sit at the table with them and eat slices of home baked rye bread spread with their own butter and jam while my rucksack was packed with butter, eggs, fat bacon and ham. Then I had to get back home without being seen by the Volkssturm patrols. (The Volkssturm was similar to the Home Guard). I didn't have much to worry about at that time in the morning but I was careful all the same.

In the summer of 1944 the programmes were interrupted for a special announcement. The Allies had attacked the Atlantic Wall but they had been driven back by the watchful, gallant troops. That was another success to cheer. We were sure the Atlantic Wall would keep the enemy at bay but the older generation pursed their lips and did not give 'any expression of hope'. The feeling at home was one of worry and I put it down to concern about the business but I grew to understand that their concern went much deeper than that. The news continued and we heard about pockets of foreign troops being mopped up and thrown back into the sea. While these reports were constantly interrupting the radio programmes, so the air raids increased both in strength and number. Wave after wave of mainly American bombers flew over in daytime raids with hardly any challenge from the Luftwaffe, most of which were grounded because of lack of fuel. At night it was the British and Commonwealth planes that flew overhead targeting industrial sites deep in the south east and southern Germany where the old heavy industry had been re-located. We soon learned that the allied invasion had come to stay. Then in July, there was an attempt to assassinate Hitler. He was only slightly hurt. Mass arrests and executions, hysteria and witchhunts followed.

Hitler had declared total war and mobilisation on the Home Front. Now the Hitler Youth really did come into their own. I joined the fire service as well as the Naval Hitler Youth. I now had two additional uniforms. My naval one was similar to the British with its bell bottom trousers, striped collar and a cap with two ribbons down the back and a hatband which read 'Marine Hitler Jugend.' My fire service uniform was of a thick and fire resistant, browny green material and a black steel helmet with a leather back flap as protection against falling, burning material..

The naval H.Y. had been fun, learning about knots and rowing and swimming and occasionally a visit to a ship. Now I learned the use of gas masks and how to couple up hoses. I knew what to attack with water and what to leave alone.. I learned about bombs and how we had to deal with different types. We had a fire pump which would normally have been on a vehicle but, with the shortage of fuel, we had to push and pull it to the danger spots. All we had were spades and buckets, push and pull power and a pump and a couple of elderly men who were too old to help but had enough voice to tell us what to do.

There were many other ways we had to help, for instance collecting up the propaganda leaflets that the allies were dropping and hand them in to our Hitler Youth leaders. We collected firewood and were told to keep our eyes and ears open and report any antiwar talk or protests. We became willing informers on a nation that was becoming more and more disillusioned. One of the things that made our task difficult was the many foreign workers. We couldn't understand them and they couldn't understand us. We had been taught to look down on a lot of these people as inferior non Aryans. Now they were our helpers!

School was chaos. Huge classes were the rule with evacuees and refugees swelling our numbers to be taught by one teacher often taken out of retirement. We did learn much, a lot about how to survive, cadge and scrounge but not much else. Most of these growing teenagers were ill fed and badly slept, disrupted and disruptive, mixed up to say the least, but all of them believed in the ultimate weapon that our Führer was having prepared. It was this that was going to win the war.

By the autumn, this pretence of victory could no longer be believed. The American troops had reached the borders of the Reich. Wounded soldiers were telling us stories that did not tally with those that were told on the wireless. Yet we still had hope. On sunny days, we could see the vapour trails as V weapons were fired at Britain. This is what our Führer was telling us would bring total victory.

Christmas was a non event. Food was very short. The black market provided only necessities. No supplies were coming in. Money was useless. Barter was the order of the day. Prunes featured largely in our day to day diet. The German army had depots for certain foods in different towns. We had a prunes depot. Many ways were devised to disguise the prune but it isn't a fruit that you can do a lot with.

Germany was shrinking. Russians were already over our border and although we had launched the Ardennes offensive, which dominated the wireless for a few days, we had been unable to keep the allies back. What was going to happen to our country? What was going to happen to us? We were told to hang on. The ultimate weapon to solve it all was coming. We in the Hitler Youth still believed this. Meanwhile at home, we had moved down into the cellar. Oma and Opa had made it as comfortable as possible but there was no disguising the tension, the thinking of what was going to happen. We had three families in our cellar. Access to it was through a trap door in a passageway to the shop and down a flight of stone steps. There was one light bulb but the electricity would often fail, especially when there was a raid, so we used candles. We had stores of potatoes in the cellar and vats of sauerkraut which gave off the smell of bad cabbage. We played endless games of cards and board games and waited. Even down there, we could hear the drone of the aeroplanes. Upstairs was dark and gloomy. There were no cars on the road because there was no fuel. Some bigger trucks had been fitted with wood gas burners and we would see them on the road during the day. Military vehicles were getting fewer and fewer and few German fighters ventured into the air. Meanwhile we waited, either for the miracle of the ultimate weapon or an invasion by the enemy.

We had to use wood on our kitchen range. Coal was no longer being delivered. All food was now local, We had to rely on what we could grow or what we could exchange for goods from the shop and there was the black market. I still went to the farms above the forests in the early mornings for food. Once I had climbed above the castle, my only contact with the town was the Church clock but once I had cleared the treeline, I could not even hear that and I was on my own. I would often find leaflets dropped from allied planes and I was supposed to collect them and hand them in but there were so many of them that I had given up.

It was our turn to have our ration of firewood from the municipal timber yard in early February. I set off with my four wheeled wooden cart to fetch our quota and took my place in the queue. An air raid was in progress. It had started at the end of January and simply carried on. I don't think the all clear ever did go. We heard planes going overhead but didn't take much notice. They had become the background to our lives. But when we heard the pitch of their engines changing, we left the shelter of the shed and went out to see what was happening. We saw them peeling off from the formation, one by one, and diving towards the town. We ran and hid behind the wood piles, looking out through the gaps in the shed wall. We could hear the roaring of approaching planes along the river and see the plumes of dust and smoke where they had dropped their bombs. The explosions were coming nearer. Then all hell was let loose, flying wood and dust was everywhere, collapsing buildings, people screaming and calling out for help. A bomb had fallen on the big shed and exploded. I felt something falling on my leg and saw my left hand shattered. A finger was ripped open and bleeding. My jacket was torn open at the front and my trouser leg was ripped above the knee. I felt no pain, only numbness and confusion. I must have got up and wandered into the open not knowing what had happened. Someone saw me, bundled me into my own hand cart and pushed me the quarter of a mile to the town's convent hospital. I can't remember it clearly. It all seemed to be in a dream. I came to as I was wheeled into the operating theatre. I was clutching my bloody hand with my handkerchief for a dressing.

Then the planes were back again, Mustangs and Marauders and

they were shooting at anything that moved. The windows in the theatre had already been shot out. A rubbish bin full of air raid debris stood beside the central table. We sat on benches round the walls, shocked into silence.

"Der Nächste," the blood spattered surgeon shouted above the din of the whining planes and the whimpering patients.

It was my turn. I climbed on to the table as best I could with a nun helping me. The surgeon took a quick look at my leg and announced a mild flesh wound. Then he looked at my stomach. That was nothing much and was patched with plaster. Then he looked at my hand. By that time, ether had been dropped on to the cotton wool and I was counting. I think I counted to six before I slipped into oblivion. I came round and saw my bandaged hand and arm. "Right, get down. Next one please." I climbed down and dropped my arm. I immediately felt a warm surge in my hand. Nobody had told me to keep my arm up or given me a sling. The stitches had burst. But time was short.

"Quick, back to your family," I was told.

I made my way past crying people and heard distant shouting and explosions. I must have spent ages wandering home through utter chaos, broken glass and bombed buildings, clouds of dust and dazed people. What a welcome I had when I reached home. There were hugs and tears and demands to know what had happened.

The following days were agony. The burst wound went septic and the only treatment was to burn off the rotting flesh with a pencil like stick. I nearly passed out each time the nurses had to use it. There was no relief for the pain. It was excruciating. Total war had come to me.

One good thing came out of the raid. The school had been bombed and that was the end of education. I couldn't join in the Hitler Youth activities, especially the fire fighting but, as soon as I was fit enough, I was able to make my way up through the Odenwald Forest to get food. I had time now to look around me and I would often be away for three or four hours at a time.

Soon after this air raid, I was presented with a bronze medal for being wounded in enemy action. It was pinned on my Hitler Youth tunic as a reward for suffering for the Fatherland and our Führer. Had I lost a limb, I would have received a silver medal and, had I lost two limbs, I would have received a gold one.

Air raids were now more intense than ever. Leaflets and anti radar metallic strips were everywhere. Refugees, mostly with farm carts pulled by emaciated cattle or horses, made their way through the town heading for central Germany fleeing from the advancing troops in the west. From the east, there was an even more frantic scramble as people tried to get away from the advancing Russians. Handcarts and horse drawn wagons served as makeshift ambulances.

Early one Spring morning, the town was rocked by an almighty bang. We could see the River Main throwing up huge waves and we rushed towards it to see what had happened. There had been no planes flying overhead so we knew this had not been caused by a bomb. Then we saw that the bridge that connected the old town with the newer northern town had been blown up. Only the archless, stone pillars pointed forlornly to the sky. Pieces of a bullock cart hung on one pillar and on another sat a dog. It stayed there for three days before someone managed to get across and rescue it. We stared at the scene in front of us, lifeless bodies and pieces of debris floating down the river. We watched with horror as a woman with a dead child in her arms and blood pouring from her body swam for the shore shouting for us to help her child but there was nothing we could do and the shouting stopped as mother and child sank beneath the surface and were washed downstream as well. All German bridges had been wired up ready to be blown up if the Americans advanced. A local S.S. detachment had blown the bridge without warning anyone what they intended to do, not even telling the people on the bridge or the farmers driving their carts across. It was all pointless. I kept dreaming of that scene. I still do now sometimes.

There were few local people out on the streets. Most of them were like us, sheltering in their cellars with the shutters on their windows closed. Enemy planes still flew overhead but there were no more raids on the town. The wireless was our main source of news, still reporting stories of attacks and counter attacks but we saw the refugees making their way through the town. We knew the hunger and saw the suffering in their faces. We knew the war was drawing to a close and wondered what would happen to us. We could hear the sounds of gunfire and rocket launchers and knew the Americans were drawing nearer. Propaganda had warned us about cannibal, American Negroes and we were in the American line of advance. How would they treat us and what about the foreign workers that were in the town? Would they turn on us when the Americans freed them for the way they had been treated ?

There were no hand painted eggs that Easter, no doughnuts or small sweets. Instead there was anxiety. It was Holy Week but there were no Church services. Instead we stayed hidden in our cellars hardly venturing out of them. Thursday came and with it an eerie silence settled over the town. There were no more planes flying over us. We heard the rumblings of distant tanks, artillery and rocket fire. In the afternoon, observer planes flew over us dropping leaflets that invited us to surrender and warning us that the town would be obliterated if we tried to defend ourselves. I rushed out into the street and collected a handful of them and took them back to the cellar for the family to read. They weren't playing games now or talking, they were sitting waiting in frozen silence.

A single aeroplane flew over on Good Friday, dropping a letter addressed to the Bürgermeister. In it he was told to hand over his town without resistance. If a single shot was fired, the Americans would send in their Artillery. One man, preferably the Bürgermeister himself, was requested to go to the west of the town with a white flag to surrender his town.

We waited. But I grew impatient. I ran up the steps and stood in the doorway looking out ignoring the women's calls for me to return to the safety of the cellar. I saw the Bürgermeister walking down the centre of the empty road. He was carrying the white flag. He did not look to left or right as he went. Nothing else moved. There was no sign that any other living thing existed. I watched until he disappeared from view, then went and told the family what I had seen.

We waited in silence. Then I went back up to the doorway and looked out. Nothing moved. It felt as though the whole world had stopped.

It was a long time before the Bürgermeister returned. He walked back up the cobbled street with the same dead expression on his face. There was no sound and no movement. He disappeared and everything was still. Then we heard the tanks rumbling and they were coming nearer and, suddenly, there was the rat-tat-tat- of a machine gun firing. Someone was firing at the Americans from above the castle. Then came the noise people in their cellars had been dreading, artil lery fire, probably ten shells in total- whistle and explode, whistle and explode. Then silence

Another lone plane flew over and another letter was dropped. If another shot was fired, there would be a bombardment.

The Mayor walked along the road again, carrying the white flag of surrender. His face was drained of all colour. He looked as white as the flag he was carrying. I watched as he walked the length of the road and I watched as he returned some time later. The women in the cellar had given up shouting for me to go down where it was safe. Nothing happened. Everywhere was silent and still. There were no more planes, no more shooting, no more noise of advancing tanks. The whole town seemed to be in limbo.

Two other boys came and joined me in the doorway and we stood there looking out at this silent world. Then we heard the sound of tanks starting up and, at the same time, we saw our first enemy soldier. He came round the corner from the Schwarzviertelgasse (Dark Quarter Alley), the first American soldier, a figure from hell. He was tall and broad and dressed from head to foot in camouflage with a helmet pushed on the back of his head that was covered in camouflage netting. He had a sten gun in his hand which he was holding more like a swagger stick than a weapon and he was draped with all the trophies of war. He had German cameras hanging round his neck and watches adorned his left arm, several of them, one above the other and he was black., the blackest man we had ever seen on the films or anywhere. And he was chewing. We stared at him in horror. We didn't know anything about chewing gum then.

Then he started coming down the road and he was coming towards us. Our families were shouting up the stairs by this time, calling for us to go down and join them but we couldn't move. We were frozen to the spot with this huge, frightening figure coming towards us. We couldn't take our eyes off him. He was the original bogey man, the devil himself. But he wasn't walking straight. He staggered from one side of the road to the other. Then his eyes fixed on us and he came straight towards us. I wanted to get away from him but I couldn't move. I stood there quite mesmerised by this huge, black man lurching towards us.

"Schnapps," he called out and made signs of drinking from a bottle, "Schnapps".

We couldn't help him. We didn't have any Schnapps. We didn't know what to say to him but we didn't have to bother. He shrugged his shoulders and staggered on and round the corner, oblivious of the fact that he was the lone invader of a terrified town.

Then they came, the real American soldiers and we shrank back against the wall. You didn't argue with these men. They came down on either side of the road in single file and they were aware of everything in their path. Round the corner came their tanks and soldiers fanned out across the market square. They were all black and we knew in an instant that we stopped believing what we had been taught, that blacks were inferior to us Aryans. These were men and you didn't belittle or laugh at them.

They searched the houses. Locks were shot off doors to allow immediate entry and windows smashed, rejected souvenirs were thrown out of windows.

People came out into the square. They looked white and frightened. They didn't speak. The American soldiers meant business. If they told you to move, you moved. Their officers were white and there was hate in their eyes, hate and revenge and they were Jewish. These men could have been the relatives of the very Jews that we had chased down the streets and whose shops we had sacked and whose synagogue we had wrecked. We had nothing to say.

The Americans Arrive

Notices appeared everywhere. Groups of silent people gathered to read what they said. They were written in both English and German and left no doubt as to what we could and could not do. We would get out of the way when American soldiers went by. There was a determined air about them. They weren't people to question. I realised that the guest workers had got out of our way in the same way that we did the Americans but we had looked at them in a different way, as if they were inferior. The white Americans looked at us as if they disliked us, almost hated us.

The days went by. It was a time of anxiety and tension and uncertainty. The tanks began to move out and more troops arrived with their lorries and jeeps, their music and supplies and gum, their whiter than white bread and numerous candy and chocolate bars.

My family started talking about the benefit of having cared for me throughout the war. They had saved me from being sent to an internment camp. They had given shelter to this English boy. Hildegard was delegated to take me to the military government H.Q. which had been established in the synagogue that I had helped sack in 1938.

We knocked on the door and waited. An American voice drawled, 'Enter', and we went in. We were face to face with the first American with whom we were going to speak. His military cap was pushed to the back of his head. His medals reflected in the light. A cigar stump was wedged in the corner of his mouth and he was chewing. He was leaning back in his chair and beside him sat Heinz, my ex Hitler Youth section leader, a quickly de-Nazified clerk and translator.

"Hi, Limey, what you doing here?" were the American's first words to me.

I looked at him in total bewilderment . "Was haben Sie gesagt?" I replied. (What did you say?)

My translator quickly took over and explained the situation to the American sergeant. He obviously impressed the officer that, although I was English, I spoke or understood very little. He had only just lied himself into the job of translator and wasn't going to lose out on this opportunity. The interview went on through him. Forms were filled in and papers signed. We eventually emerged from the building that had many, many memories for me. Memories that I knew would have caused the officer to treat me very differently had he known that I had helped to desecrate this very building.

We made our way to the Landratsamt, (District Council Office). I had to apply for a foreign national's passport. We were handed the application form and then discovered that I needed two photographs and that caused difficulties. There were no luxuries of any kind and that included films but somehow we managed to get two photos and returned to the office. There was a frantic search for a foreigner's passport. No-one had travelled abroad in the last few years. They were sorry. They had no passports for British nationals. I would have to be French. They were the only passports they could find. The details were filled in and the passport marked 1/45. Despite all the words being in German or French, my nationality was marked English. The official picked up the stamp and looked at it. It depicted a laurel wreath and a swastika. He looked at it for a while then took his pen knife from his pocket and cut the swastika out. He realised that was a mark that would not have been appreciated when I returned to England. The passport was stamped and der zame Engländer was reborn.

One of the first benefits of this transformation was felt. I was allowed displaced persons rations. Apart from that, nothing changed.

Our life was more difficult now than it had been in time of total war. We weren't frightened of the Americans but we were wary of them. We were not important. That was how we felt. There were no early morning runs to get food. American patrols were everywhere and their rule was to shoot first and ask afterwards. We became adept at bartering. These dreaded black soldiers became our firmest friends. They were a softer touch than their white comrades. We exchanged all kinds of Nazi souvenirs for chewing gum, white bread, sweets or coke. Cigarettes were good currency, not that the soldiers ever gave us any but we would dive for the stubs when they threw them away, unpick them and roll them into new cigarettes. We traded in used stamps, fake wine, anything. We had plenty of time on our hands. There was no school, nothing much to do except scrounge. German money was useless. Bartering was the order of the day. Shop shelves were empty but something could always be found if bread or meat were offered in exchange.

One day Opa Sauter asked me to help him bury a tin trunk in the garden. It contained all the family papers from before and during the war, party papers, Nazi membership cards and Nazi awards. We didn't want the Americans to find them. We spent a long time getting it buried. We weren't the only family hiding or destroying our papers.

Then came the day that changed everything. Everyone was to be allowed 60 new Deutschmarks. This was the new currency. For one day, every one was equal. We had money to spend. There were goods in the shops again. The economy had started to recover.

In July a Mercedes staff car, with a flag flying on the bonnet drew up in the market square. A British soldier got out. He was looking for Paul Briscoe. He arrived at the shop and all Opa could understand was the repetition of my name. The soldier did not speak German. Maria rushed up to the American H.Q. for an interpreter. The soldier had been sent to find me and make sure that I was fit and well and to inform me that some time in the near future, a car would come to collect me to go home. He seemed to think I would be pleased to hear this but I wasn't. I was horrified. I had never thought of going back to England. It was an unknown country to me and I didn't want to go. Miltenberg was my home. I didn't want to leave it and the family didn't want me to go. They wanted me to stay and take over the business. Hildegard and Seppl didn't have any children and they considered me their future. There was no news of Seppl. We didn't know where he was but if and when he did return, he had made it clear that he had no intention of working in the shop. I had no family in England. There was only my mother. In any case I couldn't speak English and I didn't want to go. The soldier drove off and I pushed the whole idea to the back of my mind.

Gradually reconstruction work started. There were no new materials and everything had to be salvaged from the old buildings. Fathers and brothers were returning home and there were many reunions but there was still no news of Seppl. He had been listed as missing in action but that could have meant any number of things. Hildegard knew all about the affairs he had and was convinced that he would turn up one day. The two of us were very close and I looked on her as my real mother. There was talk of school starting again. We were slowly getting back to normal when the dreadful day in October arrived. The same black Mercedes car drew up in the market place. It was a different soldier but the same message. This one was smart and brisk. I had half an hour to collect my things. I would then be taken to the British Consulate in Frankfurt.

It was pandemonium. We had learned that when the allies said half an hour, they meant half an hour. We had thirty minutes to collect everything that I wanted to keep of my childhood and everything that I would need in the future. I didn't have a chance to say I didn't want to go. I was going back to England, to a country I didn't know and a mother I couldn't remember.

Hildegard was rushing around gathering my clothes together. My every day clothes were the ones I had worn in the Hitler Youth. All the insignia had to be cut off quickly. The women had it in their minds that all Englishmen played cricket and golf and wore plus fours, so in went a pair of plus fours. I don't know where Hildegard found them but they were by far the largest item in the case. I would need my school books, so in went my history and geography books which, of course, were all about Germany. I added my Hitler Youth certificates and record book. I was proud of those and what I had achieved. I didn't want to leave them behind. I even had a Tyrolean hat with a shaving brush kind of decoration on the side added to my possessions. They thought British men wore bowler hats and this was the nearest they could find to one. This was all going on amongst wailing and crying and supplications to God. By the time I was escorted out to the car, I was crying as well. A crowd had collected in the square to see me off and I didn't want to go. I think it was one of the worst moments in my life, saying goodbye to the people and town that I loved and had come to consider my home.

At least they spoke German in the British consulate. The soldier who had collected me from Miltenberg tried to talk to me but we couldn't understand each other and he soon gave up. I didn't want to talk. I was too mesmerised by the speed with which my departure had happened. They seemed to understand at the consulate and they tried to reassure me. They told me my relations would be waiting for me in England and there would be a red carpet laid out for me. But I wasn't going to England just then. I would have to stay in a displaced persons camp until there was room for me on a plane. They had to have

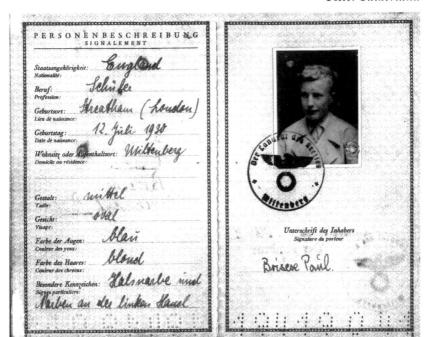

Passport issued in Germany the Clerk cut the Swastika out of the stamp with his pen-knife

me near the airport as I would be leaving without notice. They would get me back to my mother as soon as possible. They told me that I would be comfortable in the camp and that there were thousands of people there like me, waiting to get back to their homes.

I had visions of going to a hotel or a guest house like Mother and I had stayed in when we first came to Germany. I couldn't have been more wrong. The camp was a vast estate of flats, line after line of blocks of flats. I was driven there by another soldier in a big black car. We stopped at the third block. The soldier lead me up flight after flight of stairs until we reached the top floor. Thirty people were already there. Most of them were sleeping on their beds. Some were smoking. A few were drinking. A group were playing cards or talking or arguing and I couldn't understand a word any of them were saying. There were several different nationalities there and as many different languages. I was shown the bed in the corner. The soldier said something to me I didn't understand and left. I was on my own in bedlam.

I hated the place. Nothing was private. Nothing was safe. They shouted. They fought. They swore. They drank. They danced. They snored. They made love. I cowered in the corner of the room or pre tended to be asleep. I seemed to be there for ever, thinking of my family in Miltenberg and longing to be back there with them. I was rescued by an English family. Somebody must have told them I was there and they came looking for me. They too were waiting to be repatriated. Fortunately they could speak German. They made a space for me in their room and I moved in to their block. They explained to me what was going on throughout the world and, especially, in Europe. I started to see things in a different light then and realised that I wasn't the only one with problems. Although I had lived in Germany and saw myself as a German, they told me things that I had not been aware were happening. I was only there four days when there was a knock on the door and a voice calling out, "It's off to England for you, my boy."

The black car drove straight out to Frankfurt Airport and the waiting Dakota. It was full of soldiers, mostly British but there were some Americans. I was shown my place on a slatted wooden seat and had my seat belt fastened. I sat there with my precious case between my feet. I felt cold and frightened. When the plane took off it sounded like a thunderstorm. It was so noisy that it was impossible to have a conversation but some of the men did shout to each other. One or two of them shouted to me but I couldn't understand what they were saying and they soon gave up. I held my ticket and papers firmly in my hand and wondered who would be there to meet me. Then we touched down with a bump and taxied towards the buildings of Croydon Airport. A lot had happened in the eleven years since I had last seen them. We climbed down a ladder to the ground and made our way to the hall. The soldiers all had kitbags. I held on to my case tightly. There were a few people waiting in the hall. Some of the soldiers were met but nobody seemed to be looking for me. Gradually everyone disappeared and I was left there on my own. I clutched my case tightly and wondered what to do. I looked round the huge space. There were a few chairs and tables scattered around but no people and no movement. I was home.

I waited there for a long time. Then I went and stood on the pavement outside watching out for someone who might be coming to look for me. It was November and it was cold and damp and foggy. It grew dark and I stood there not knowing what to do. The lights were blurred by the fog and everything was damp. A policeman walked by and nodded at me before he walked on. It was some time later that the same policeman returned. This time he stopped to talk to me. I think he was asking me if I was alright but I didn't understand what he was saying. I tried to explain in a mixture of German and the few English words I had. I gave him my papers and he took me back inside the airport to study them and, eventually, he managed to contact my mother.

England 1945

The policeman explained to me with a mixture of sign language and simple words that I should wait in the airport. My mother was going to collect me. I waited. I could have sat on one of the chairs but I stood with my case beside me and waited. The fog seemed to permeate into this vast hall, dimming the lights. Then there was the sound of running feet. Two ladies came through the door and I didn't know which was my mother. I chose the prettiest and I picked the wrong one. I picked my mother's friend Molly. I could see Mother was hurt but she soon covered it up and started talking. Fortunately they could both speak German although Mother's was limited. It seemed she had been told I was coming home but nobody had let her know when I was coming. I started to answer but they hustled me outside and down the road to the bus stop. They didn't want to miss the last bus. It was a long time coming. The fog was so thick by this time that I didn't see it until it loomed out of the darkness almost on top of us. We seemed to be travelling through streets for a long time. Molly got off two stops before we did. We carried on to Harrington Road and walked down to number 72, along two rows of identical houses, their gables breaking through the swirling fog like miniature mountains and I thought longingly of the hills that I had left behind in Germany. We climbed three flights of stairs and mother opened the door to a shabby room. She switched on a two bar electric fire which gave out some heat.

"Which is my room?" I asked.

"This one," she said. "I only have the one room. I'll put a mattress on the floor for you. I'll tell you when you can go to the bathroom. We have to share it with five other families."

I stared at her. "Why do you live like this?" I asked. "England won the war, didn't she?"

That was when Mother started to tell me what her life had been like during the war. She had spent most of it in prison and she kept saying she had done it for me. She had sent information to Germany and she seemed to think I should be pleased.

I was horrified. Only criminals went to prison. How could my own mother be involved in anything bad. I suppose I was tired and disappointed. I hadn't expected England, the winners of the war, to be like this. I longed to be back in Miltenberg with my German family.

Mother asked me if I was hungry. I asked her if she had a kitchen.

"No," she told me. "I eat out and you'll have to as well, but I have some bread and cheese" She turned the fire on it's side and toasted the bread with the cheese on top and I had my first English meal,- Welsh rarebit, Harrington Road style.

The next morning, Mother and I walked along South Norwood High Street. We went along roads of identical houses with the occasional gap where a bomb had fallen until we reached a big, old Victorian house where Molly lived. That was when I met her husband Richard. He had grown up in the Gorbals area of Glasgow and, although he could speak some German, he spoke it with such a strong Scottish accent, I couldn't make head or tail of what he was talking about. He had always championed the Nazi cause and supported Sir Oswald Mosley. He had become a blackshirt before the war. Molly had heard him addressing the crowds at Hyde Park Corner, urging them to join the cause and she had stayed behind to talk to him. That was how they met. They had lived together ever since but they couldn't marry because Richard already had a wife and family in Glasgow.

Richard was a painter and decorator by trade but he was more interested in politics and people's rights than anything else. As a member of Mosley's Unionist Party, he was opposed to war with Germany and had refused to fight. So he had been arrested and interned on the Isle of Man under Section 18b of the Defence of the Realm Act.

At the start of the war, Mother worked as a journalist for the Ministry of Information. She would tell Molly and Richard of secret documents she was finding, such as the movement of arms through Turkey and other countries. Richard had managed to find a friend who was interested in this and said that he would like to meet her. This 'friend' invited Mother and Molly to his flat where they could pass over all this information. Mother hid nothing. She told him about every aspect of her work. Then the police came in and the two women were arrested for treason. They could have been sentenced to prison for life. Molly owned some property and she sold it and briefed a King's

Counsel to defend them. He managed to get them reduced sentences. By the time the war was over, both women were out of prison on parole. They had to report to the police regularly and couldn't move out of the area without permission. This was an episode of her life about which my mother refused to talk but there were parts which she couldn't hide from me. I found it very difficult to come to terms with what she had done. Mother was always one to act first and think afterwards and I began to wonder if I ever would settle down in this strange country with my lively mother. It was all so different to the organised, settled life I had had in Miltenberg.

I still felt German yet the English people looked on Germans as the enemy. I must have looked German. I didn't have any English clothes. I would often hear comments when I went by and I was sure they were directed at me. I can still remember the catcalls that followed me down the road when I wore my plus fours with the pork pie hat on my head. I didn't understand the words but I understood their meaning.

I had no wish to speak English but I had no choice. I found it a very difficult tongue to master.

I moved in with Richard and Molly after a few days. They had a bigger room than Mother did and they curtained a corner of it for me so that I did have a little privacy. I went to work with Richard each day, washing down the walls and filling in the cracks. I'd never done anything like that before but I soon learned. As the days went by, his Scottish accent seemed to grow stronger and I would get a headache from trying to understand him. We went to a real dive of a workmen's cafe for lunch each day. The boss behind the counter had a wooden leg that clonked to the hatch to order, 'Two more sausage and mash and two roly polys with custard.' Large steaming mugs of tea were poured out - we never had coffee. Sugar was stirred with a stained tea spoon that was chained to the counter.

Then Mother found a small flat in Croydon and the two of us moved in there.

The flat was in Limes Road and we were lucky to get it. Soldiers were returning home, desperate for anywhere to live. People who had been bombed out were looking for new homes. Bombed properties had been shored up and people were living in them, even garages had been put into use as temporary homes. Mother and I couldn't expect any priority but she worked for the local paper and got to hear of any vacancies before they appeared in print.

I had never met anyone like our landlady. She was always cleaning. She whitewashed the front doorstep and polished everything that could be remotely polished. She used gallons of bleach everywhere until the whole house smelt like a public toilet. She had been a barmaid and played the piano as if she was still playing to a crowded bar, very loudly. Plaster busts of Mozart and Handel gazed down from the shelves behind her. From time to time she would burst into song at such a pitch that her voice drowned the sound of the piano. She was very nice to me but she was horrible to Mother. I was obviously too old to be a war baby but she seemed to think mother hadn't been married when I was born.

I spent hours on my own with only the landlady's musical renderings for company. Mother was always out reporting local affairs, weddings and council meetings. She was particularly busy in the evenings and at weekends. I stayed in the flat and thought of my life back in Germany. I didn't dare go out on my own because I was frightened that I wouldn't be able to find my way home and people wouldn't understand what I was trying to say to them. I was lonely, hungry, frustrated and homesick for Germany.

Mother worried that I was spending so much time on my own. One day she came home all pleased with herself. She had found a German club in the town and it was going to meet the following Thursday. I was excited about the chance to speak in my own tongue again. I couldn't wait for Thursday. Armed with details of how to find the club and which bus to take, I set out. It was in a Church hall. There were lots of people there, mostly older than myself but that didn't matter. They made me welcome and asked me about myself and I told them. I told them about the Third Reich and Hitler. I told them what I had done in the Hitler Youth and about the guest workers and the Americans taking over the town. Then it dawned on me that it had grown very quiet in the hall. Everyone was listening to what I was saying. They were all looking at me and I saw the looks on their faces and the penny dropped. They were Jewish. They were German Jews who had escaped from Germany before the war. I stood up and walked out. I felt angry. I blamed my mother. Why hadn't she warned me? Why hadn't she checked who all these people were?

I had to sort myself out. It was no good sitting in that room all day and feeling sorry for myself. I realised I was missing the comfort of

Church and determined to go the morning service that next Sunday. Nobody told me about the different religions that were practised in England. I didn't know anything about Methodists and Baptists and Jehovah's Witnesses. I went to the nearest Church and took my place in a pew. As soon as the service started I was lost. Why weren't the prayers being said in Latin? How could they be good Catholics when the altar was not prepared and the priest was in his every day clothes? I didn't recognise the hymns until the chords were struck for the third one. It was, 'Glorious things of Thee are spoken,' my German National Anthem. I stood up and sung it as I had sung it back in Germany. Perplexed members of the congregation turned and looked at me as I sang out, "Deutschland, Deutschland über alles...." I didn't care. It made my day and I felt much better as I made my way back to the lonely flat.

We sat down and talked. Mother asked me what I wanted to do and I told her I wanted to be an architect. That was fine and she made appointments for us to see several architects but none of them wanted to employ me unless Mother paid a fee for me to be articled. In any case they would be reluctant to take a German boy, especially one that couldn't speak English. That was the end of my dream. One of the older architects had suggested that I should go to College and take a course on the History of Architecture with basic drawing and technical drawing as an extra, so our next port of call was at Croydon College of Arts and Crafts.

It was a very strange interview. I was surprised when the principal invited me to go and sit beside him on his side of the desk and started to talk about life classes and modelling. He said that I would make a good model and he started to stroke my arms and legs. I had never been in a situation like this. I guessed this was how the English held their interviews. I wasn't sure I was correct in my understanding of what he was saying. I was learning some English but it was very limited. I presumed it must be alright because, after all, he was the head of the College but I eased my chair a little further away from him.

Soon after I started at the school, he and one of the teachers invited me to go to the ballet with them in London. I had expected some other pupils to go as well, but I was the only one. I felt very uncomfortable with the two of them especially as they were kissing and hugging all through the performance. I tried to avoid looking at them. Everything about this country seemed so strange and so different to Germany. I presumed this was how people did behave in England.

It was Sundays that seemed really strange. Everyone went to Church on Sunday morning in Miltenberg. In England, a lot of people didn't go to Church at all. They seemed to worship their little cars or motor bikes instead. You would see them washing and polishing them until they shone.

Newspapers were different too. They told what was happening all over the world. Some of the tabloids showed gaudy pictures and told stories that would never have been written in Germany. And, as for the newspaper sellers, I couldn't believe they would leave piles of newspapers with a hat or tin beside them for people to put their money in. I couldn't believe that the British were so honest. But what worried me most was the anti-German propaganda and details about the concentration camps that appeared daily. I didn't believe the stories they were telling. I didn't want to believe them. I thought the British were trying to stir up anti-German feelings. We hadn't known anything about these camps in Germany. I was quite convinced that had they existed, we would, at least, have heard rumours about them.

Then there was the bomb damage. Somehow I hadn't thought about England being bombed. There seemed to be far more damaged buildings here than there had been in Germany. People were living in the ruined buildings and wild flowers grew where houses and cellars had once been. Back home, reconstruction work had started before I had left. Germans wouldn't have lived in these conditions. It took me a long time to appreciate all the problems that the English were having to face and their responsibilities to other nations. It was years before I realised how much of the allied effort had to go towards reorganising the rest of the world or understood the effects of the Treaty of Versailles and the political and economic miracle stimulated by the Marshal Plan.

I was now a full time art student and I loved it. I had my own clothing coupons and bought a pair of baggy corduroy trousers so that I looked like the other students. They were the fashion of the day. I also had a brightly coloured shirt and scarf. A new Paul Briscoe had been born. The atmosphere was so relaxed that I managed to blend in easily. My guttural attempts to speak English were almost an advanto tage. Then an art student took me under his wing and I made my first friend. Ron took me home with him and I met his family. They lived out at Addington and they made me welcome. Their house was so different to the tiny flat Mother and I shared in Croydon. Ron had a brother and sister who were older than him. We all got on well.

I was doing well at the school as well. I loved drawing, especially drawings of buildings with their details, styles and perspective. I was happy, especially as Mother had found another flat and we were able to escape from 30, Limes Road.

The new flat was the first in a long line of weird places that Mother managed to nose out. She heard about an international club through her work on the local paper. It offered board and lodging at a very reasonable rent. We couldn't believe our luck but we soon found out why it was so cheap.

Our landlord, Terry Driscoll, was Irish. He had bought up a number of Victorian houses and converted them into bed-sitting rooms. He hadn't spent much on the conversion or on the furniture either. Mother's bed was two tea chests with a mattress laid on them. Mine was even more ramshackle. He had provided the bare minimum in each room. There were basic heating and washing facilities. Anything else had to be provided by the tenants. These were people from all over the globe, mostly coloured people who had come to England to be educated on the recommendation of their governments in fields that would be beneficial to their own countries when they returned. The British government had appealed to people to help these students with accommodation. Terry Driscoll was one of those that responded.

I had never met people like it. Some of them didn't know what electricity was or how to use a toilet. That was where I came in. I was suddenly in demand. I was the unpaid maintenance man, boiler man, dustman, gardener and general factotum. I was needed and wanted and even admired for my help. Most of this help was a crisis management job. One night, Mother and I couldn't get to sleep because the toilet in the next room to us was being flushed repeatedly. I got up and went to see what was happening. The floor of the toilet was awash. One very dark African student was standing on the toilet seat and, as soon as the water overflowed, he was pulling the chain again.

"I'll fix it," I told him.

Climbing on to the toilet seat, I felt into the cistern and moved the ballcock. The water stopped.

"What you done?"

I told him I wasn't sure but the water wouldn't bother him again. He wanted me to look at his room so I followed him downstairs. Three Africans shared the room and water was pouring through the ceiling. They had gathered all their belongings on to the beds, themselves as well. Everything was wet, their beds, their belongings, their hair.

"All O.K.," their friend said. Big, wide grins appeared on their faces. I was their friend for life.

The staff were all young Irish girls who had never been away from home before. They were lonely and naive. So were most of the residents. Two of the girls lived in the basement next to the boiler room which was my domain but they got on well together, perhaps too well. I went past the doorway and, looking in, I saw two pairs of moving feet, one white, one black. I beat a hasty retreat.

There must have been three hundred of us living at the club in a number of houses, all of them packed to the roof. People would appear from nowhere, weaving their way along paths and through gardens to the main block at mealtimes. Meals were pure theatre. The water jugs would be passed round but many drank straight from the jugs rather than pour the water into the glasses. Bread and butter would be piled high on the tables only for it all to disappear before everyone had sat down. Tired waitresses would keep replenishing the plates until everyone seemed satisfied. Our Irish landlord stood at one end of the room staring over the scene like a benevolent father figure. He may have been a rogue but he was tolerant. A lot of the local people objected to these strange, often uncouth but helpless people. He tried to ease their lot whenever he could. He tried to help me.

Terry found some of his residents wanted lessons in German conversation to further their studies and he introduced them to me. They were mostly Indian but it brought me in a small amount of money. The first student was fine but the second student was not. He insisted that the lessons took place while we were walking in the park. That was alright by me. Then he wanted to increase the amount he paid me but I told him that I was quite happy with what he was giving me, but he was insistent. One day when we were walking through the woodland part of the park, he lunged at me and tried to pull my trousers down. That certainly wasn't part of the agreed German lessons. I ran all the way back and told Mother what had happened. She told me about the problems some men had with boys and how lonely these young men were a long way away from home. I hadn't thought of that but I didn't bother with German lessons after that. But it made me think of other instances, particularly back in Germany where some of the monks had showed unusual fondness to us boys and would often have a particular favourite. There was one young priest that we all admired but we kept our distance from him.

It was while we were at the club that my mother told me I would have to leave the College and get a job. She could no longer afford the fees and I needed to earn some money to help financially.

I was thunderstruck. I loved my life at the Art School. I had a good friend in Ron and had fallen in love with his sister although she didn't know of my feelings. I felt I was really growing into a young man of the time. I had my fashionable clothes. I had been given extra rations when I returned as a displaced person and that included extra clothes coupons but I also received clothes parcels from the Canadian Red Cross donated by lumberjacks and golfers. I suppose I sported a mixed up style of dress but it went down well amongst the future artists. I couldn't believe that it was all to end. I turned on my mother. I told her that she could not treat me like that and that mothers didn't do that sort of thing. I ranted and raved but it was no good. There wasn't the money for me to carry on at the Art School.

I hadn't any idea of the job I would like to do and I didn't care either but Mother searched the advertisements in the local paper. She found one that she thought would be suitable, 'Wanted: Young boy, 15 or 16 required as assistant groundsman at South Norwood Sports Club. Phone...... for details and interview.'

Mother made all the arrangements but as the day of the interview loomed, she told me that I would have to go on my own. I set off not knowing what to expect. I had the usual piece of paper in my hand directing me to bus stops and listing the numbers of the buses I needed to catch. I thought there would be several people there but there was only Don the groundsman. I was to work under him. He was a simple soul. That was revealed by his interviewing techniques.

"What's your first name."

"Christopher Paul."

"I'll call you Chris."

I'd got the job. Then he told me what my duties were, grass cutting, turfing, brushing and rolling the tennis courts, marking out the cricket square.....

"Vat is cricket?" It took me many months before I discovered the answer.

I worked hard and long hours too, preparing the courts and the bowling greens and the pitches but I didn't mind. Don was a good man to work for and he worked just as hard himself. People often stopped and talked to me and, although I was beginning to understand more, I still couldn't hold a conversation. So I started going to English evening classes and I was lucky because I had a sympathetic teacher who gave me a lot of encouragement. I began to look forward to my lessons with her and started to read newspapers and simple books.

But there were many issues that still confused me. People who knew my background, often asked me why I hadn't suffered at the hands of the Germans. They often repeated stories of the bestialities and details of the death camps, stories that I had great difficulty in believing. They wouldn't believe that those of us living in Germany had no idea of any of this. I would often retaliate by asking about the bombing of our cities but I didn't have to look far to know that England had suffered in the same way from our own Luftwaffe. I found it difficult to put my thoughts in order and to relate it to everything I had learned in Germany. Unfortunately my Mother was working every evening so I had to sort it all out for myself.

I had some holiday to come and Mother suggested I went to stay with her parents, my grandparents. She hadn't spoken about them very much and it turned out they had cut her out of their thoughts and life when she was sent to prison. I was the means of them getting together again. I was the lost grandson returning to the fold. I was spoilt. It meant so much to me to find a family of my own. They lived in Wallasey in Cheshire in one of a row of neat, bow fronted late Victorian houses in Seaview Road. They were a strict Catholic family, Victorian in their outlook. I can remember endless journeys on clanging trams and going to Liverpool through the Mersey tunnel and walking on the bleak, windswept beaches. The week was soon over and I had to return to the world of work in South London but it wasn't to be for long.

Mother decided that she was fed up with London and her hack journalist job and she wanted to get out. We now had papers spread all over the floor with mother on her knees searching for any suitable work that would get us away from the life we were living. She found one that looked suitable. It was for a secretary to a famous writer and editor of a literary magazine on the Suffolk/Norfolk borders. There was also work available for a young man to work on the arable farm. Mother wrote and had an immediate reply, "Come and see me. Will meet train at Diss. Bring son. P.S. will refund fares."

I had no idea where Suffolk was. Suffolk or Siberia was all the same to me. We set off from Liverpool Street station. There was a car waiting for us at Diss. Mother knew who to look for. The writer was famous enough for that. He welcomed us and was really friendly. He told us that he was a farmer as well as a writer. We were driven through water meadows and low lying marshy land to the village of Thelnetham. We arrived at a big village farmhouse that was flanked by two huge beech trees. We went straight to the office where they discussed the work and terms. I was to be the farm-hand at a wage of ten shillings a week from which seven shillings and sixpence would be taken for board and lodging. My mother was to do all the literary and secretarial work but nothing to do with the farm. We could start as soon as possible. We went back to Croydon to make arrangements for our new life in Suffolk.

Nothing had prepared me for what was to come. Neither Mother or I had ever experienced anything like it. I suppose I had grown up a bit since I had left Miltenberg and I had begun to appreciate the difficulties that Mother was experiencing. She found it difficult to get work at all and, although she tried to get back to journalism, she was always given the most mundane jobs on small local papers. Whenever she applied for a post, she was asked what she had done during the war and that was generally the end of the interview. She had to work fantastic hours for very little money. She was a happy go lucky person by nature but she had reached the stage where she couldn't see any future in staying where she was. Suffolk offered both of us the chance for which she had been looking.

The farmer-cum-writer lived with his third wife and a daughter in a big house some way away from the farm. A secretary and friend of the farmer's wife lived in a cottage near the farm. Opposite that was another cottage in which the farm foreman lived with his family. Dougal was a red haired, mightily tall Scotsman who worked day and night. Working seemed to be the sole purpose of his life. Paul the cowman lived in a cottage down in the village. He was a family man. The rest of the workers all lived in the three storey farm house. There was Gladys the middle aged (to my eyes) ex-landgirl, Harold the horseman, who had a dry wit and was often cynical but very reliable and helpful, Johnny the tractor driver and mechanic, Phyllis the housekeeper, Trevor the poultryman who was a keen horse punter and seemed to know more about horses than poultry. And then there was Franz, a German prisoner of war and ex-farm blacksmith. He was the only one who really knew about farming and I often wondered what he thought about the set up in Suffolk. He stayed at the farm during the week and returned to the Prisoner of War camp each weekend. There were two others, a man with a glass eye and a boy worker who had been to a free expression school and didn't seem to know what life was about. Added to this, the workers often had friends or relations staying with them, so it took a long time to find out exactly who did live in the farm house. All of them, except for Trevor the poultry man, were conchies, conscientious objectors who refused to do military service so had been sent to do farmwork instead. This was the community that Mother and I joined.

I was so pleased to meet Franz and have a chance to talk in my own language again. He was the only true farmer in the whole outfit and must have wondered about the farming methods of the English. All of the others worked hard but they lacked skills and basic farming knowledge.

We all ate together in the big, bare kitchen on the long scrubbed table. The housekeeper fed us on an endless supply of cheap food, most of which seemed to be based on Yorkshire pudding ; Yorkshire pudding with vegetable stew or with corned beef or cheese flan or egg salad. We rarely had meat or sausages. She had been seen at the local post office sending large parcels and we often wondered if our loss was someone else's gain.

Mother spent the days at the main house and I didn't see a lot of her except for the evening meal and often there would be more work

Lodge Farm Thelnetham on Suffolk/Norfolk border in 1946. Back Row (l to r): Farm Secretary, Farmer/Writer, his wife. Front Row (l to r): Me, Franz (German POW), Farmer's daughter, Gladys (Ex Land Girl), My Mother

Lodge Farm 1999

be done afterwards. I sensed that her writer was not the character she had expected him to be and that the job did not come up to her expectations. Soon after we had arrived, we were all invited to the big house for our first 'service'. We all wore our best clothes. It was the cleanest I had ever seen them. We trooped into the main room where John, the farmer, was waiting wearing a carpenter's apron and sandals to look like Jesus Christ. Carpenter's tools and wood shavings were spread out on a long, rough hewn table. A wooden cross was in the middle of the table along with a large, old fashioned wooden jack-plane. When we were all seated, he would start praying. One of the workers would read the lesson. Then the farmer cum writer would give us an address and a blessing and we would be free to go back to the farmhouse, to our Sunday lunch of small amounts of meat and vegetables and large amounts of Yorkshire pudding. These services became a regular part of our lives.

Dougal would be out working before we started each morning. At ploughing time, we would see his stark figure on the skyline urging on the horses with bloodcurdling oaths in guttural Scottish. What he didn't achieve with brain power, he achieved through brute force

Johnny, the tractor man was an intellectual and a beautiful piano player. Beethoven's sonatas would waft through the house deep into the night. Gladys doted on him and she would sit listening to him with a rapt expression on her face. I once met Gladys in the corridor in the middle of the night with a candle held high. She said she was going to help her troops in the Crimea as she went by. Nothing surprised me there. I saw Gladys driving the farm's ancient Bedford lorry one summer's day and she was stripped to the waist. She was quite unconcerned but I nearly went into the ditch with the horse I was leading when I saw her. Women didn't behave like that in Germany.

Yet I found a sense of peace in Suffolk that I hadn't experienced anywhere else in England, a similar feeling to the days back in Germany when we were being bombed and I would climb above the castle into the quiet of the German countryside. I didn't know anything about farming but I was prepared to learn. My work on the farm was a daily excursion into the unknown. One hot summer's day, I was sent out with Maggy, the Suffolk Punch mare hitched to a hay rake. Dougal came out with me and showed me how to row up the cut of the now dry hay ready for baling. It looked easy. I sat up on a sprung metal seat that shot up and down as we went over stones and mole hills. I held the reins in my hands and had been told to pull on the side when I wanted the horse to turn but I hadn't been given any guidance on horse language or control. It was getting hotter and hotter and the flies were bothering the horse. I sat on the bouncing seat urging her to go langsam (slowly), links (left) or rechts (right). The horse by this time and not understanding German, was fully in con-

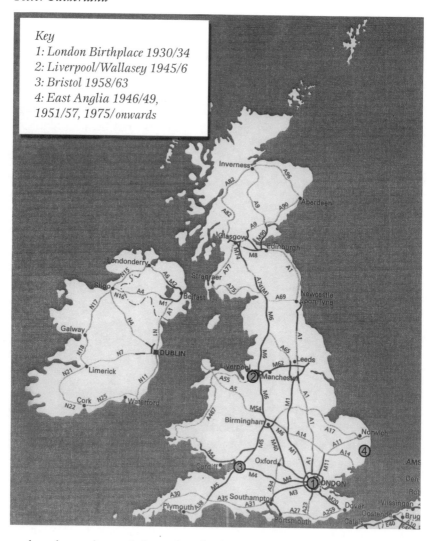

Key
1: *London Birthplace 1930/34*
2: *Liverpool/Wallasey 1945/6*
3: *Bristol 1958/63*
4: *East Anglia 1946/49,*
1951/57, 1975/onwards

trol and set about doing what had to be done at top speed. I was sitting up on the hayrake seat looking down at vast curved tines that were gathering up the hay. I pressed the pedal to force the tines up, leaving the gathered hay in a long straight line ready to be baled, leastways, that was the theory, but the hay emerged in a rather more haphazard fashion, sometimes in huge lumps and at others as thin wisps. We seemed to have finished the field very quickly. The horse wanted to go into the next field. There was no doubt about what she

MAP OF EAST ANGLIA

wanted to do. She charged at the gate at as near a gallop as any horse would with a heavy hay rake in tow. The wheel hub caught on the gate post and the horse reared. I and the hay rake were thrown into the ditch and the horse galloped off into the beet field with parts of the shafts still hanging on to the harness and started to tuck in.

I slunk off to the farm to find Franz. Any of the others would have laughed but he didn't. He gathered up some tools and came back with me to catch the horse and sort out the damage. He also gave me a sound lesson on controlling a horse, emphasising that the horse must always know who was the master and then it will do what you want it to do. I did admire Franz. He was always ready to help. He had a slow, quiet way of working and he was always so practical, always careful and always reliable.

It was just after this that I was sent into the covered yard to look after a dying bullock. He was kept away from the other animals by hurdles. His breathing was sharp and rasping and his eyes were darting wildly from one thing to another. I was left with him. The only light came from an old oil lamp hanging from a beam in the roof. I had to give him drinks of water and drops of linseed oil from a bottle. I stayed with him all night, sleeping on the straw as best I could but when I woke up, the restless eyes had stopped wandering and were staring straight ahead. The bullock was lying dead in the first morning light. I stayed there when the knacker man came. He cut it up in the yard there and he seemed to pull out miles of colourful gore from its inside.

I had another job to do with the horses in the autumn but, this time, Franz came with me and got me started. I was to harrow a field of winter wheat after it had been sown. This time it was sheer pleasure, a feeling of power and peace as

Paul unloading mangolds in Oak Tree Meadow with Bobby 'helping'

the horses plodded backwards and forwards leaving a beautiful soft tilth around the sides and headlands in double bouts or rows to make a really satisfying job.

Franz was a good friend. My English was still limited, so it was great to be able to talk to someone in my own language and who understood me and the way I had spent my childhood. He treated me as an equal, sometimes a bit too much of an equal. I was going into town one Saturday and asked him if there was anything he would like me to bring back. His request made me blush to my hair roots. He was having a relationship with an English girl and wanted some contraceptives. Off I went on my ten shilling bike for my afternoon off, a fish and chip lunch and the afternoon in the cinema. My problems started in the chemist shop. My attempts to be served by the man failed, instead a young girl cheerfully asked me what I wanted. I looked at her in horror. Franz had made his request in German. I knew the German word for contraceptive but however could I describe such a thing to a young girl? I stuttered and the girl waited patiently. Then it came out, Please can I have a balloon for a man? There was a quick consultation with the chemist, then she asked if it was for me. No, no, it was for a friend. I received the packet and dashed out of the shop and hoped that Franz would ask someone else to do his shopping for him in future.

I felt sorry for the German prisoners in the camp. After all, the war was over but they were still being held as prisoners although I must admit none of them seemed particularly worried. I didn't realise that they were being kept here until their own country was ready for their return and there would be jobs and homes for them. Some who lived in places that were now in the Russian zone did not want to go back at all. I didn't appreciate that, I was sure they would be missing their own homes with Christmas drawing near, so I asked Franz if there was anything he thought they would like. Would they like some chicken for Christmas. He thought that was a good idea so I waited until it was dark, then made my way to the chicken house. They had so many hens in there but I was sure they wouldn't miss a few. As I went through the door, the birds panicked. There was dust and feathers and squawking hens everywhere. I seized half a dozen and shoved them in a sack which was pretty difficult because those that were in the sack were fighting to get out as I tried to add another. I managed to get away but the string must have come undone as I went through the hedge and there were protesting chickens caught in the hedge and I couldn't catch them. By this time the dogs at the house were barking. I went and fetched Franz. He came straight away and despatched each of the hens with a quick pull of the neck - easy.

Christmas was a dull affair. There were no decorations, no celebrations. We had a good meal and then people dozed while the strains of Beethoven's sonatas came from the front room.

The two bright lights in my life were Franz and Margaret, who came up from the village to help in the house and was really friendly. Her father was known as Digger Thurlow because he used to dig the graves in the local churchyard. I was in real luck when Mrs Thurlow offered me board and lodging for five shillings a week. I was two and six-pence better off and much better fed. Soon after I moved there, Digger was taken ill and I was delegated to be Digger Briscoe. There was only one grave to dig so I didn't start it until lunchtime. I didn't think it would take me long but I hadn't reckoned on the Suffolk clay, chalk and flint stones. I came across bones and bric-a-brac about teatime but there was still more digging to do. I was still digging when it grew dark and the owls began to fly. Digging a grave in a remote, country Church on my own is not something I would recommend. I was cold, hungry and frightened and determined that if I ever had to dig an-other grave, I would start earlier in the day.

I didn't stay long with the Thurlows. Mother was on the move again and I went with her. The job hadn't turned out as she had ex-pected and the writer-cum-farmer was eccentric to the point of being odd. Mother had seen a job for an assistant warden at a Land Army Hostel advertised in the local paper. She applied for it and was offered it at the interview with a request that she start as soon as possible. She lived in on the job but I had to find digs for myself and I needed to find a job to pay for them.

My digs were very basic. I provided extra income for the family so I felt an intruder into their family life. Both the parents worked lo-cally, the mother being the barmaid in the local pub. Stoke by Nayland was in a lovely part of the world. It was high above the Stour valley with spectacular views. The Church stood on the highest point of the village and its dressed flintstone walls shone out over the distant Con-stable countryside.

I wanted a job to do with architecture. I felt that this was the time for me to think of my own future. I had never lost the ambition I had formed back at Miltenberg. I scanned the papers looking for some-thing suitable and found an advertisement for a job with Essex County Council Town and Country Planning Department. I was invited for interview and set off with my drawing folder from the Art School in Croydon under my arm. The interview must have gone well because, despite my difficulty with the language, I was offered the position of

A visit to Constable Country 1948

junior draughtsman.

I was elated. I couldn't wait to get back and tell my mother. I had got myself a job, or so I thought. Two days later, a letter came for me from Chelmsford. They were very sorry but they would have to withdraw the offer of the job. Having looked at my application, they had realised that my call-up for National Service was imminent. What was this all about? I didn't know anything about National Service. I cycled over to see Mother and a council of war was held with Richard and Molly who had bought a house in the area. Richard knew what to do. I would have to register as a conscientious objector. I was an ideal candidate to avoid National Service.

I was bewildered. What was a conscientious objector? That took some explaining but it seemed the answer. Mother asked what would happen if they didn't accept my application.

"Don't worry," Richard told her, "he can go and live in Southern Ireland and stay there for a few years."

"If I don't go into the army what do I have to do instead?" I asked him.

"Oh, work on the land or in a hospital or something like that," Richard said airily.

I was having serious doubts about Richard's ability to solve every crisis. But there had been another event which meant I really needed to delay going into the army or preferably put off going in altogether. Mother's father had died and left her a small legacy. Mother wanted to invest it and she was thinking of buying a row of four cottages that Richard had found. Molly and Richard lived at Monks Eleigh in West Suffolk. We went and stayed with them for a few days to look at these cottages. The two of them came down with us to see them and Richard advised mother on the value of them. We couldn't understand why the asking price was so low, £175 for four timber framed, thatched cottages. We soon found out. They all had demolition orders on them. Three were occupied but the middle one was empty. We visited the Council offices where they confirmed that the cottages were scheduled for demolition but we were also given guidance on how this order could be lifted on two of them. We decided they were worth buying.

"Paul can do them up while he's waiting to hear from the Tribunal," my mother said.

But there was likely to be two or three months before all the paperwork was signed and I could start on them. I had to find myself a job for the time being. I found one for a gardener/handyman at Polstead Country Club. I applied for it and was appointed straight away. I don't think anyone else wanted it and I soon found out why. I was expected to do everything. The owner had many grandiose ideas and a mind

Paul at Christopher Cottage 1948/49

befuddled by too much drink.

The country club was in a big Georgian hall between the Church and the pub. The first thing the owner showed me when I arrived for work was a big hole that had been dug at the side of the hall. That was to be the swimming pool. He told me I could carry on digging it out in my spare time. Then he showed me the pigs in the stables and the chickens. They were to be fed with the leftovers from the kitchen and I had to keep them clean. Then there was the kitchen where I was expected to help with the vegetables and the washing up and I was expected to clean the guests' shoes which they would leave outside their doors for me to collect and return. Then I was expected to act as the waiter for breakfast and lunch and clear the tables afterwards. The kitchen gardens and greenhouse were half a mile down the road. I was expected to tend those as well and bring the produce to the house. Cutting grass and fabric maintenance were also mentioned but, by this time, I had stopped listening. I did ask about the rest of the staff. It seemed that Mrs Carter came up from the village to do the cooking and a girl helped her and would occasionally help with the waiting and washing up. Other than that, it appeared that I was to be on my own.

I tried but ideas of having a completed swimming pool soon went out of the roof. It became a long list of chores from the minute I set foot on the place. Take the swill to the pigs, muck out, back to the kitchen and try to remember to take my mucky boots off before putting on whites to serve the breakfast. Try to wash my hands. Clear up and wash up. Take the orders from the kitchen for vegetables. Rush to the garden, dig up vegetables and rush back. Check rat traps under the beds but make sure the visitors were out of the room first. There were one or two awkward instances when I hadn't checked carefully enough. Clear out the empties from the bar, - Sir and Madam were generally too far gone to do this themselves. Sometimes, when they were having a 'do', I would have to carry Madam to her bedroom. She would be too far gone to realise what was happening to her. Sir generally collapsed beneath the bar along with his white Alsatian that was in the same state as his master. One night, when they were having a social evening, the boss came out from behind the bar and tripped over his dog. They both slumped down where they fell and slept. I pushed and shoved them into a dark corner and left them to their slumbers and took over the bar. The whole set up was chaotic. There were always extra jobs that needed doing, grass to cut, with a push mower of course because the motor one had broken; prepare the stalls for the village fete and anything else that came to mind.

There was one happy relief though. Stoke by Nayland was the next village to Polstead and there was a German Prisoner of War camp in the hall there. I used to see and stop to talk to the Germans and I got to know several of them quite well. One of them asked me if I would like to go to their camp to see a film one day and, when I asked what it was, they told me, 'Spiel im Sommerwind.' I stared at them in disbelief. They couldn't believe it when I told them that I had been in that film. That was how for the first time I saw myself in the film that had been made back in Miltenberg. It made me feel homesick for Miltenberg. Although I was still settling down in England, I still longed to see Germany again. I used to save my sweet coupons and send gifts back to the family and they wrote to me regularly but it wasn't the same as being there.

Then the sale of the four cottages had been completed. They were ready for renovation. I had a hammer, a Woolworths's saw, a pair of pincers and a ruler. I was ready to start work.

We stayed with Molly and Richard at first in Monks Eleigh. They were buying run down properties, doing them up, selling them and moving on to another. I would bike down to our cottage each morning and get on with the job.

I decided to start on the middle cottage. We couldn't even get into the cottage because of the undergrowth so my first job was to clear that. The cottages were basically well built, timber framed with wattle and daub infilling. Most of the work involved stripping off the old paper and distemper and replastering and filling in the cracks and holes. The walls were filthy dirty and a lot of glass needed to be replaced. Water had to be connected to the sink with a new rotary pump. Richard was a great help. He was always ready to give advice and I needed it. I got most of it sorted out indoors and we moved in three weeks later. Then it was outside work to our own and the other three cottages. It was mostly repairs to the roofs and guttering.

A gypsy family lived down the road and they had a daughter called Dolly. She was quite capable of looking after herself. I found her very disturbing because her behaviour certainly didn't adhere to the Catholic principles I had been taught. To Dolly, life was there to be enjoyed. It was the way she enjoyed it that bothered me. I met, or should I say was waylaid by Dolly on a couple of nights as I went back to Molly's house after a day's work. That was the cause of the confrontation with Dolly's fiery mother. She stood at our front door with her legs apart and her arms akimbo wanting to know what I was up to. I was to leave her daughter alone or there would be trouble. This episode kept Richard amused for days but it taught me a lesson.

It was about this time that the four of us became involved in a local Church. Kettlebaston was about two miles from Monks Eleigh. It was set on a dominating ridge overlooking the River Brett. I never did find out how we managed to meet up with Father Butler but meet up we did. He was the priest to a lovely old Suffolk, flint Church with wall paintings and treasures from a richer age. The one thing that Father Butler did not want was a congregation. It was HIS Church where he could commune with HIS God. We were certainly outsiders and the locals were suspicious of us but we liked singing and both Mother and I had a Catholic background. Father Butler was a very high Anglo Catholic and he needed a choir. He had a devout harmonium player-cum-server. The four of us were all he wanted. We would have a weekly choir practice in the organ player's house and then, with clouds of incense, liberal brush swirls of holy water and ringing bells, the service would reach its climax in the Eucharist prayers with more bells and incense. In all the time we were there we were never disturbed by a congregation of even one. Father Butler was happy and completely unaware of his spiritual isolation.

Then I received a summons to appear in front of a tribunal at Fulham Town Hall. It was to adjudicate on my conscientious objection to doing National Service. I was sent a travel warrant. I went in fear and trepidation down to Fulham. I didn't know what to expect although Richard gave me plenty of advice. The instructions I had received advised me that a team of four would hear my case, a solicitor, a County Court judge, a Trade Union official and a theologian. I knew it would be a test of my understanding of English and also their ability to interpret my pidgin variety of it.

It was pathetic.

"Why don't you want to fight in the army?"

"I do not want to fight no more. I have seen enough war and I am up my nose with the war."

I meant to say that I was fed up to my back teeth with war but I didn't find the right words. The theologian asked me several questions which I couldn't answer because I couldn't understand them. The others fired questions at me. How could I explain my sincerely held views when my vocabulary was so limited. I felt completely frustrated.

What other verdict could they have given. "Case dismissed. Objection overruled."

I was given a document that contained their verdict and also details of the method for lodging an appeal.

I went home feeling crestfallen. I had to admit to myself that I had been put up to the whole idea by Richard and it was Richard that persuaded me to lodge an appeal. That was another torture I had to endure and once again the case was dismissed. I was told to report to Ipswich for my medical examination preparatory to call up. There was one good thing that came out of the whole exercise. I had had an extra two months to work on the cottages and, in that time, most of the essential work had been done. Mother applied for the demolition order to be lifted and, after many letters and appeals, the council gave in.

Then my call up papers came with a travel warrant. I was to travel from Ipswich to Barford Camp in North Yorkshire. So once again, I set off for the unknown.

National Service

I had never experienced anything like it. I knew all about the German army methods. I had learned it all as a Hitler Youth and watching the German soldiers on manoeuvres or on the newsreels at the cinema. The British army wasn't like that at all. Nothing had prepared me for what was to come.

I had set off on a special train from Kings Cross station and from the second I stood on the platform, I was bemused. I was one of what seemed like hundreds of young men all uncertain about what was to come. There was an assortment of dress and an assortment of backgrounds. I had a barrow boy on one side of me from the East End of London who spoke broad cockney of which I understood one word in ten. It was like a foreign language to me especially as he kept lapsing into rhyming slang. On my other side was a young man who had been to public school and spoke as if he had a plum in his mouth and who I found equally difficult to follow. I was feeling worried because I thought that I might get a lot of anti-German feeling when these other recruits knew my background. They didn't take long to find out but there was no bad feeling. It caused them a lot of laughter and I was the butt of their jokes for a while.

The train arrived at one long platform and our baptism of fire started. We were to be trained by a cavalry division of the armoured corps and they were tough. There were twenty lance corporals waiting on the platform for us, each of them smart to the tips of their toes, wearing cloaks and carrying whips.

"Come on you shower of humanity. Fall in and follow us in order," was the shouted command as we filtered out on to the platform.

We arrived at the large, forbidding barracks. Flags were flying and the entrance and pathways were lined with whitewashed concrete blocks. This was our new home. We were herded to the main square. Orders and obscenities flew in all directions. Lists were produced and shouted out. We were divided into groups of even numbers. Then we were frog marched off to be issued with fatigue kit, boots and gaiters, a grey overall type uniform for training and rough work, underclothes, shirts, beret, belt. We didn't get a chance to tell him our size. The sergeant eyed us up and we were issued with clothes that were roughly our size. We didn't argue. Then came the most important part of the day, we were issued with our numbers. I will remember mine until my dying day, 22123499.

Climbing holiday in 1948

We were allocated sleeping quarters, the corporal shouting a mixture of orders until each of us was lined up with a bunk bed.

"Ten minutes," he shouted at us, "and I want to see you outside, lined up, in your new clothes. Get a move on. At the double, you human filth."

By this time we were bewildered, hungry and dead miserable and these obscenities only made it worse. There was a mad rush to get changed and out within the ten minute deadline. Some of the men didn't know what gaiters were and had some odd ideas about where they should be worn. What came out of the huts beggared description, a horde of human misery with hanging, ill fitting clothes, laceless or half done up boots, misplaced gaiters, berets that wouldn't have stayed on top of the head if it hadn't been for the ears. Then at the double, we were urged towards the square. Now the sergeants and officers took over. They were standing on a raised platform and, with oaths and inhuman language, ordered us into lines of six. It took some time. We were ordered to be silent but it was an unnecessary order. We were too bewildered to even want to talk, even the East End barrow boy was dumb. Then came a short address about our purpose there. Like it or not, we were to be made into a fighting force that had always made the English soldier the best in the world. A quick glance along the lines would have reassured any future enemy. Then we were to have our first drill. We were to march round the square in our present formation.

Then came the order to forward march and a mass shuffle forward started. Some who had been in a cadet force marched properly, but not me. That was one thing I did know, how to march and I set off with a very smart goose step. The reaction was immediate.

"Who's that ****** Kraut in the ranks. Does he think he's in the ****** German army?"

I had to step out and tried to explain that I came from Germany. From then on, I was a marked man. The Segeant always called me kraut and loved making fun of me. That was the trouble with most of those N.C.O.s. They had a warped sense of humour. But my comrades weren't bothered about my nationality. They were a pretty mixed up bunch themselves so that helped.

We were marched to the mess at the double for our first meal in the army. It was awful. Big splodges of food were almost thrown into our mess tins, over-cooked and lumpy but it was eaten all the same because we were ravenous. Prunes and custard and a huge mug of stewed tea added to our welcome of National Service hospitality,

Then we really got down to basic training. Up at the crack of dawn, shaving in ice cold water, washing at long metal troughs, boots polished, hair cut so close that we were almost bald, still hungry after cold porridge and congealed fatty bacon and sausages with mountains of thick white bread and we were out, ready for the day's torture.

There was parade, P.E., field training, assault courses, carrying people heavier than ourselves through water, then change into full uniform all at the double with square bashing on the central parade ground to come. Then there was weapons drill, learning how to salute and how to stand stock still at attention. Then there was the sudden order to be back changed for P.E. in ten minutes. We sweated and we cursed. We wanted to throttle the corporals and sergeants who bullied and swore at us. We would be asked questions and be told to shut up when we answered them. Every day, our tormentors thought up new swear words and new torments. We were being broken and trained to obey. Unfit boys were driven on. It was inhuman and degrading but slowly the purpose of it all was being achieved. The odd word of praise showed that the officers were not the inhuman people we had considered them.

Church parade, army fashion was another trick. We assembled in the square where all Church of England were ordered to fall out to the left. Most of the men were C.of E. Then the non conformists fell out and were marched off. I was one of the Catholics and we found ourselves being marched not to the Church but to the kitchen where we had to peel potatoes for the Sunday lunch. We did better than the Salvation Army and the Jehovah's Witnesses. They had to clean out the toilets. That was the last time I was a Catholic. The following Sunday, nearly everyone was C.of E.

The sergeant never forgot the way I had marched, goose step fashion and he had it in for the kraut which is what he called me. One day, after we had changed from P.E. and reassembled on the square, he demanded to know where the smell was coming from. He found his way up to me and demanded to know if I ever washed. I told him I had just showered but that wasn't good enough for him. He ordered two corporals to take me along to the showers and get me clean which they did with scrubbing brushes. They scrubbed my legs until they were raw.

Another time, he came and stood close behind me, so close that I could feel his hot breath on the back of my neck

"Kraut," he said, "am I hurting you?"

"No, Sir," I said.

"Kraut, am I hurting you." he repeated.

"No Sir."

"Of course I am," he shouted. " I'm standing on your bloody hair. March this man away and get his hair cut," he ordered.

That was my second hair cut in less than a week.

But the basic training did end. It ended with the dreaded Passing Out Parade. Our drill, our shaves, our uniforms, our haircuts all had

National Service (TA) 1950/51

to be perfect. Every brass button had to shine and our boots had to be lovingly spit and polished. The threat was always that if we failed, we would be returned for basic training again. None of us wanted that.

We marched behind the regimental band. We formed up in long open order for inspection. Officers with their canes and followed by the sergeant major walked up and down the ranks. We were then ordered to close ranks and stand at ease. The officer then addressed us as if we were human beings - what a change. We marched again, past the saluting platform and, as soon as we were dismissed, made straight for the NAAFI and celebration. We were soldiers.

Now came the important part. We were being posted. We had filled in forms stating any preference we might have and describing any skills we had. We really thought they would be considered but when the lists went up on the board we learned how wrong we were. C.P.Briscoe 22123499 was destined for Egypt. Some were going to Hong Kong, others to Austria, Denmark, Germany, anywhere where British influence needed troops. The weeks before the draft was due out, I went down with flu. I was taken off the list until I was fit. The next list that went on the board sealed my fate, - C.P.Briscoe 22123499 to North Germany. I was going home. I was going to be in the 7th Armoured Division, the Desert Rats that had been made famous in

North Africa under General Montgomery.

I returned to Germany with mixed feelings. Part of me still thought of Germany as my home but now I was going as a member of the British armed forces. I didn't know what to expect. We had a ghastly journey in a troop ship across the North Sea and eventually arrived at the barracks. We were amazed at the comfort that had been provided for the German soldiers. They were large imposing buildings surrounded by grass and trees. There were good washrooms, central heating, small dormitories and roomy dining rooms. They were a contrast to our old barracks back in England.

We were detailed into groups for our basic training. I was in the light armoured reconnaissance unit of Daimler armoured cars and Dingo scout cars. Each vehicle took a team of three and each of us had to learn two of the required skills. I was to be trained as driver and wireless operator. It all went well and I enjoyed it. We would often travel far from camp and I was seeing a lot of Germany that I didn't know. We even patrolled the Russian border, the Iron Curtain as it had come to be known.

It was back in the barracks that I found myself most useful. I could speak the language and I understood the Germans. I became the go-between for all the shady deals between the German civilians who worked on the camp and the soldiers who had things to sell or exchange. This included cheap cigarettes, coffee, tea, chocolates and nylons, all things that were virtually unobtainable in post war Europe. They were currency. I was the one who was asked to negotiate exchanging these goods for services and gifts that the soldiers wanted.

I wrote love letters for them to the many shady ladies that patrolled outside the main approaches to the camp. It was strictly forbidden but a thriving trade nevertheless.

Then there was a check in the barracks and the goods in my cupboard were revealed.

Trading in this way was a court martial offence even though I was not making a profit from it. Everything I had was confiscated even though it did not belong to me and I was given filthy cleaning duties. I had to lie low. I don't know what would have happened if the Education Officer had not realised why I had become involved and how well I understood the German mentality and the language. I was transferred to Field Security duties to the old German cavalry barracks at

Germany Gosclar - National Service BAOR

Goslow with a distant view of the Brocken, the highest peak in the Harz mountains. It was all so much more relaxed. I could walk about the town in civilian clothes and mix with the local population so as to pick up any information. Nobody trained me in any way or advised me on how to avoid trouble. I suppose it all went to my head and I became over confident. There was one occasion when I went to a meeting of a right wing ex Nazi movement. I had been asked to report on the speeches. That meeting took me back to the wartime reports and party meetings that we used to hear on the radio. Some of the audience shouted approval. Others muttered and questioned the sanity of the speaker. I should have kept my mouth shut but I didn't. I declared it was all rubbish. Someone near me heard and pointed me out to his neighbour. I heard him muttering that I was an English soldier who would make trouble for them. Several men started to round on me with threatening gestures and I had to beat a hasty retreat. An ugly looking guard was standing in the doorway and he almost caught hold of me but I managed to get away. But it left me scared. It was a reminder of the Beerhall days of Hitler in Munich.

A similar thing happened to me at a Communist rally in Hamburg while on leave there. Luckily I was rescued by a military police patrol who bundled me into a jeep and drove off at speed. The situation had been turning threatening. The war was over but there were still Germans holding on to their old beliefs and still seeing the English as the enemy.

There was an army leave centre near Goslar at Bad Harzburg. These centres also attracted their share of ladies. I should have learned my lesson but with my knowledge of German I felt the big man. I was only too ready to help the soldiers with their assignations. I don't feel any pride in what I did. My values were at an all time low.

I was doing interesting work on border control points, questioning refugees about troop movements in the eastern zone and acquiring any information that might be of value. We went on patrols but we kept well clear of the high fences and wall sections because many of them had been made lethal with electrified wire and mines had been laid alongside them. Watch towers with strong searchlights would suddenly catch us unawares. We had to be good map readers and keep on checking them. Roads would suddenly end where they had been blown up and were now blocked by concrete blocks, barbed wire and metal spikes. Some roads had the wire running down the centre of them. The Western side was well used but the East German side was overgrown and had a sinister air to it. It may have been in our minds but the feeling was there. It was a trembling peace. Doors and windows of the houses in the East were boarded up and criss-crossed with barbed wire, the villages themselves were dead and deserted and the ground around them ploughed up so that every footmark would show up to the watchful troops. Some farmhouses had their land shut off on the other side of the fence and, in some places, the fence actually divided communities. Anyone approaching the wall from the Russian zone would be bathed in an orange glow as the lights shone in their direction and then we would hear the sound of machine gun fire. Most walls in history had been built to keep the enemy out. This had been built to keep people in. We never patrolled there without a feeling of desolation and tension as if we were venturing into the unknown.

It was 1950 and I was half way through my National Service. I was feeling more settled because I had become friendly with a German family. They had two daughters and a son. They lived and worked in Goslar. They always made me welcome and it was great to have the family environment rather than spend long evenings in the barracks. Renate was the younger of the two girls and, for the first time in my life, I found myself falling in love. It was obvious that her parents approved of the relationship.

Later that year, I had some leave and decided to go and visit my foster-family in Miltenberg. Armed with an interzonal pass, I set off. I hadn't realised I should have bought a ticket as well. I produced the pass whenever I was asked for my ticket and it was duly punched, in fact it was punched so often that it was difficult to see what it was for. Arriving at the station beside the River Main, my thoughts turned back sixteen years to the time I had first stood on this spot and I thought of the good times I had spent here. I made my way to the Marktplaz with such mixed feelings. I was wearing my army uniform and many people cast sideway glances at me. I think some of them recognised me. I rang the side door bell and waited. The door opened cautiously and Hildegard was there, my foster mother from my childhood years.

"Das Paulchen ist hier," (Little Paul is here), she shouted and then we were in each others arms, laughing and crying at the same time. I was home again. There were the familiar smells of lino and furniture, carpets and glue and HOME.

We hurried up the stairs and all the time Hildegard was calling out. "Little Paul is here. Our little Paul is an English soldier and he's come home."

Maria clasped me to her bosom and Seppl came out of one of the store rooms. Everyone was talking at once. I couldn't get a word in edgeways. But first it was time for the essentials, coffee, tea, wine and that became the pattern for the next few days. Wherever I went and whoever I met produced the wine with the welcome. I began to see the world through a haze. Everyone insisted I wore my uniform. I was embarrassed about that but they all thought it was a huge joke, - little Paul who had been in the Hitler Youth was now an English soldier. I met old school friends, old comrades from the Hitler Youth, old neighbours, and we told and retold the wartime stories and with each repetition, they became more and more exaggerated.

The discussions I had with Hildegard and Seppl were far more profound. They insisted that this was my home and that was where my future lay. They had not been able to have any children. There was nobody to take over the shop. 'Your mother has her own life', they said. 'Your home and your future is here'.

I knew they were talking sense. I had no job to which I could return in England and, although I felt at home in Germany, I also felt English. I didn't even have a home in England. Mother had sold the Suffolk cottages and was staying with her sister in Hastings. I was beginning to feel trapped, trapped in a small town life and controlled by the shop. Part of me was saying, 'No, no, no', while the other was asking what was the alternative. I didn't know what to say to Hildegard and Seppl. I felt very unsettled.

Then Seppl started to tell Hildegard and me about his experiences in Yugoslavia when we were sitting having coffee. He had started serving on the Western front and had got as far as Dunkirk when he was posted to the Balkans. He spent most of his time in Albania and Yugoslavia. He had picked up the Slav language and had been installed as the governor of a small town. He was cock of the walk. He lived in the bishop's palace from which he flew the Nazi flag. He had pretty Slav secretaries and plenty of informers whom he manipulated with ease and who probably manipulated him in the way of Balkan politics. He became the big fish in a small pond. When he came home on leave, he would bring valuables with him, stamp collections, antique trinkets and fabrics. Once he had started he carried on telling us of all the shady deals he had undertaken, all the strings he had pulled. As the war progressed and the tide began to turn, Seppl who was always an opportunist, switched sides. Hildegard had been told that he was missing, believed killed. Now we learned that he had signed on with Marshal Tito's side.

I couldn't answer him. Now there had been two fallen idols in my life, first my mother and now Seppl. I was hurt and angry and that made Seppl laugh and that hurt even more.

'Why? I asked him, 'Couldn't you be like Pastor Heider?'

"You think he was perfect," Seppl mocked and then told me how the priest had been found on the ground with a broken leg late at night. He had been visiting a housewife in her bedroom and had fallen through a glass roof in his haste to escape. I had always respected the priest and now there was another fallen idol. The visit which I had been anticipating with joy was turning sour but it strengthened my doubts of staying in Miltenberg and the shop for the rest of my life.

The family in Goslar thought I was being offered a wonderful chance to stay in Germany and take over a prosperous business. They were overjoyed and enthusiastic. They discovered that all I needed was a work permit and they even went to the trouble of obtaining a form which I only had to fill in and then I would be able to stay in Germany after demobilisation. They also mentioned that Renate wouldn't have to leave Germany and she would be assured of a good future. I began to feel trapped. I seemed to have lived my whole life with a feeling of uncertainty and I began to feel that I was being forced down a path that I didn't want to go, I was being sold to materialism. I didn't see it in those clear terms then, but I was feeling uneasy.

Time was passing so quickly. The other soldiers were talking about their plans when they were demobilised. They had worries but they also had plans. For me, the future was empty but I still had this dreadful feeling of being trapped. Then it was spring and time to say good-bye to the German family. They said they would come to see me and I can remember thinking I don't know where. I had no idea where I would be living. So I arrived with our demob group at Bovington camp, the Royal Armoured Corps discharge centre. Uniforms were handed in. We had our last pay parade and I turned my back on the army. I was on my own again, an all time low, no home, no friends, no job, no future and a girl friend left behind in Germany.

Back Home

I didn't have anywhere to go and I began to wonder if I should have listened to the family in Germany and stayed over there, but Mother soon found a semi detached cottage. It was in Marlesford, a small village 16 miles north east of Ipswich. It had two bedrooms, a snug living room and a kitchen which had once been the village butcher's shop. There was a well outside the back door for drinking water and an earth closet under the stairs that led up to the landing. There was a big garden which was overgrown with waist high weeds. Our neighbours were a childless couple. They were very friendly and helpful which was very fortunate. Also he was a builder.

I set to, decorating and sprucing the place up. It was early summer so there was still time to put in some vegetables. We went to the local saleyard at Wickham Market and managed to buy the bare essentials that we needed which were delivered the same day on a small lorry. I had taken a fancy to a folding, put-you-up bed and thought it was a real bargain at half a crown. The first night I slept on it was to be the last. I settled down on my bargain and soon fell asleep. I must have turned over during the night or made some movement because, with a loud bang, the whole thing reared up, folded up and over with me on the inside. There was no way I could get out. I had been rolled up with it and was held in its iron grip. There was only one thing I could do and that was shout. I shouted. That brought Mother in and she wasn't a lot of help. She leaned against the wall and laughed until the tears were running down her face. We didn't have any tools except for a screwdriver and a hammer. When Mother calmed down, she fetched those and somehow managed to extricate me, bruised and cold. I finished the night sleeping on the floor and next morning consigned my bed to the scrap heap and bought a proper, single, second-hand bed.

I had to find a job and quickly. Mother was virtually penniless. The little money she did have left had gone on buying the furniture. I had to work to keep us both alive and pay for electricity and coal. Farming seemed the only option unless I was prepared to travel. So off I went on my second-hand bike which I had also purchased from the sale yard and offered my unskilled services. I was offered work at Hall Farm as a relief cowman and general farm-hand. From having an ordered life with too much free time, I was thrown in at the deep end. I started work at half past six, milking, mucking out and cleaning up. Then I went back home for breakfast at nine o'clock and back to the farm by ten o'clock. I went home at midday for dinner and then returned for general farmwork until second milking at half past four until six. If there was no overtime, then I had a free evening, I worked Saturday and Sundays as well. Cows had to be milked. At the end of the day, I would cycle home with my can of milk hanging from my handle bars.

Any free time was spent working at home. There were always things needing to be done in the cottage and the garden to tend. There never seemed to be a spare moment. Then, to cap it all, a letter came from Renate announcing her arrival the next day. She was coming to see what the prospects in England were.

Mother was furious. She hated cooking, let alone for another mouth with German tastes to feed. Although rationing had finished in Germany, it was only just ending in Britain and there were still a lot of shortages. Mother was going to be left with Renate while I was at work and it was at a time when she was starting to think of her own career. She wanted time on her own to write. I became the whipping boy between the two women. The only peace I had was milking the cows twice a day. I would lean back on the flanks of the unprotesting cows and dread going home to the hostile atmosphere.

One evening, instead of going straight home, I went to the small church with the square, flint tower to seek help. As I was leaving, I met the large, benevolent figure of an English country parson. Kindness and understanding was in his eyes. He introduced himself and asked if I lived in the village and I started to tell him about Mother and myself and how Renate had come from Germany.

"Shall we go into the peace of the Church," he said, "and we can talk if you want to."

He was so kind and things seemed so much easier when I could discuss them with somebody else, especially somebody who understood and was sympathetic. It was all so different to the confession box in Germany where the priest stayed hidden behind a metal grill. Mark Meynell listened to everything I said and made some sugges- tions to resolve the situation. He also offered to call in and talk to Mother.

Things were so much easier after that. Even work became easier and I looked at the conflicts at home under a different light. Renate had been with us for three weeks and it obviously wasn't working. She must have written to her mother because one day, on a very hot, thun- dery afternoon, there was a loud knocking on the door. I opened it and there was the large figure of Renate's mother. There was no cer- emony, no preamble.

"You are coming home now. You are not staying in this hole one more minute," she announced in Wagnerian tones. There was no room for doubt or dissent. "Pack your things this instant."

"Why the hurry?" I asked limply.

She didn't answer. She simply glowered at me through her heavy breathing and heaving bosom. Renate and I were crying in turn. Mother was standing at the side of the room obviously relieved to get rid of this problem. And then they were gone, her mother marching down to the waiting taxi with Renate tripping obediently behind her. They didn't look back.

I felt battered and humiliated. I hardly knew what I was doing. Then I started to think about myself and where I was going. It was July and in a few days I would be twenty-one. I felt really mixed up and a bout of diarrhoea from drinking untreated milk and the con- tinuous hard work at the farm didn't help. There was just a glimmer of light and that was a girl called Dawn. Her garden backed onto ours and she would talk to me over the fence when I was gardening. I asked her if we could see more of each other and she agreed. I invited her in for my birthday tea, my 21st. It was to be a normal working day but I was finishing at four o'clock. Dawn worked at an art gal- lery and studio in Woodbridge. I had plucked up courage and invited her in for tea at five. I had made myself a cake and iced it. It looked a bit pathetic, but I had tried. Mother made me some sandwiches and there were three small presents for me to unwrap. Then Dawn came. She had brought a present as well. Mother was very polite but I knew her and I could see that she was weighing Dawn up. Then came the explosion. Dawn looked at the cake and asked, with a snigger, why I hadn't asked my mother to make a proper cake.

I flew into a rage. I couldn't help it. I had spent such a lot of time and effort on that cake. It was the centrepiece of my special day. I picked it up and threw it into the fireplace, candles and all. It shattered and I rushed upstairs and shut myself in my bedroom. The party was over and, in the eyes of the law, I was now an adult.

The whole experience made me think. I had to get out of the life I was leading. I didn't want to be a cowman for the rest of my life. The trouble was that I didn't know what I wanted to do and the choices were limited because of lack of transport. I began to think about the building trade. There was a building firm in Marlesford so I went to see them. Because of National Service, I was too old to be an apprentice. I could become an improver which meant a three year period starting at labourer's wages. I would have to attend evening classes in Ipswich at my own expense and, subject to my passing the building construction exam and having a satisfactory record with the firm, I would then be a qualified carpenter and be paid the proper rate for the job. That was just what I wanted and I accepted there and then.

I had to be at the yard by half past seven and we were taken to the job in hand by lorry. I had to assemble my own tool kit by the end of my first year and had a half crown a week tool allowance for it. I can remember the terrific positive feeling I had when I went to work that first day. I had done something for myself. I was so lucky with the master carpenter in the firm. He was a real old fusspot but he insisted on the highest standard in everything. He always turned up for work in a spotless white apron and his tools were sharp and sparkled with oil. He was a perfectionist and an excellent teacher. His motto was, 'Do your best, if it isn't, do it again.' Stan was very tolerant but intolerant with bad workmanship. I have always been very grateful to him for the things he taught me. The firm had a contract to refurbish Framlingham School and there was a lot of overtime to get the job finished in time before the students came back in September. The wages for this overtime helped me buy my first motor bike, a second hand Royal Enfield 250cc. It was the pride of my life. Now I was mobile. I could get to my evening classes in Ipswich without any problems.

I was coming out of my shell a bit. Mark Meynell, the parish priest had kept in touch with me ever since that first meeting when Renate was staying with us and he nudged me along. We had a local squire who I hadn't met but I had met his aristocratic brother under rather unfortunate circumstances. I had been trying to chop a clothes prop out of the hedge when he had come along with his two black labradors at heel and asked what I thought I was doing and who had given me permission. I was told in no uncertain terms what he thought of townies who moved up from London and I was warned off. It probably didn't help that I took the clothes prop with me.

He didn't seem to remember the incident when I met him for the second time. The rector asked me to join the Church choir, "The Lightly and Brightly choir." It was run by the same gentleman of the clothes prop confrontation. He liked to be called Mister Dick. He had been a colonel in the Guards and he ran the choir with great gusto.

Marlesford was a lovely village in which to live but, at times, it felt as though we had slipped back into the middle ages. We still had a squire. There was a box pew at the front of the Church for him and his family to worship away from the prying eyes of the villagers. Nobody ever ventured into that pew. It was the squire's. He lived in the Hall which was surrounded by parkland, where village parties and festivals were held. That was where we had the party for the Coronation of 1952. All the children were given mugs to commemorate the occasion. Long trestle tables were groaning with food, sandwiches and sponge cakes, sausage rolls and pork pies and dishes of jelly and ice cream. Every conceivable vantage point bore a Union Jack or bunting, even the children were decked in red, white and blue. The Lightly and Brightly Choir entertained with singing patriotic songs and everyone joined in. Then there were races for the children and sideshows. I took a second or two to stop and look at the scene. It was so happy and so typically English and I couldn't help but compare it with the celebrations there had been in Miltenberg. There they had marked their anniversaries with military music and organised marches, many references to Hitler and the Third Reich.

Mother's friend, Ethne had come up for the celebrations. She was dressed as a gypsy and told fortunes. There was quite a queue waiting to consult her, mainly young men who wanted to know about their future love life. I don't think Ethne had told fortunes before but she didn't let them down. She really rose to the occasion. She taught ballet in London and now she offered to help the gamekeeper's wife, who ran the local nursery group, to perform a ballet on the front lawn. This lady threw herself into it with enthusiasm much to the vocal support of the locals but it all came to an unfortunate end. She was finishing her dying swan dance when she leaped into the air and landed heavily and sprained her ankle. She had to be carried off on a chair.

In the evening there was a dance in the village hall which was known locally as the hut. The Lightly and Brightly choir sang during the interval. Some of the farmworkers had visited the village pub on the way and failed to appreciate the entertainment, calling our sopranos shriekers and similar names.

Ethne, mother's tall and stunning friend was really warming to the spirit of the Coronation. She was having a fine old time at the back of the stage along with the local boys and a few crates of Adam's beer until one of the mothers went in search of her son and found him in the arms of that wicked woman from London. She hauled him out by his ears and marched him through the dancers announcing what she thought of Ethne to one and all. That Sunday, at the morning service, the Squire invited Ethne into his box pew!

I was being drawn into more and more village activities. Mark Meynell, our parish priest, started the Marlesford Amateur Dramatic Society, aptly called M.A.D.S. and I became one of its members. Whatever the play or the revue, it always ended up as a farce. In one production, I was the waiter and I had to wear the vicar's evening suit. The fact that he was nearly a foot taller than me didn't daunt the lady in charge of the wardrobe. I was tied, strapped up and pinned into the clothing so that I could hardly bend and walking was painful. Then, when I came to pour out the coffee I discovered that some wit had poured the coffee away and replaced it with baked beans in tomato sauce. On another occasion, I had to light a cigar for a member of the cast who sported a large moustache. It went well in the rehearsal but on the night, I lit his moustache as well as the cigar. He pulled the moustache off and threw it on to the floor and the two of us started stamping on it and dancing on the sparks to stop anything else catching alight. The audience thought it was all part of the show and laughed every time they saw us after that. When the villain made a pass at the maiden who was swooning on the couch, the leg fell off and tipped the two of them on to the ground so much for amateur dramatics!

Regular dances were held in the hut on Saturday nights. The usual pattern was for the boys to sit on the row of chairs on one side of the hall and the girls on the other. They didn't generally start to fraternise until after the refreshment interval although that could be marred by several people who fancied themselves as singers and would offer their services. Nobody liked to refuse them. They would warble on and on, until the M.C. would stand up and announce the next dance and that did the trick.

The railway was another feature of country life. We were on a small branch line from Framlingham to Campsey Ash junction connecting with the main line from Lowestoft to Ipswich. It was not unknown for the guard to shout out to someone who was hurrying along the lane to catch the train and tell him not to worry. They would wait for him to arrive and they did. There was one occasion when I was waiting for the train and it stopped short of the station. We wondered what was happening. When it drew in, the guard held up two rabbits, then walked along the platform showing them to the passengers that were already on the train. He had been checking his rabbit snares which he had set along the banks. Then there was a whistle, the train was back in business and went on to Framlingham. It wasn't to last. Dr. Beeching shut the passenger service and a few years later, the goods line was closed. The rails were taken up and it became a walk for the ramblers.

I was happy at work. I would often go out to do some of the more regular jobs on my own, rehang a door or a window, repair guttering or replace rotten wood. I had a motor bike and could get to the really remote parts of Suffolk. I had two pannier bags on the back of my bike which held my tools and any materials I might need. The homeowners would often give me fruit or vegetables from their own gardens as a thanks, especially if I did some extra job for them.

Norah Briscoe, my mother (late 1950s)

Mother was more settled. She had a small job as the local correspondent on the East Anglian Daily Times and she was saving some money so that she could go abroad again. I even had a short holiday. I went climbing in the Alps. I had missed the mountains and hills in Suffolk and it was wonderful to

94

walk in the peace and grandeur of the Alps on my own. But then, it was good to get home again.

It was at one of the village dances that I met Helmut. He had come to England to work and to improve his English. I appreciated the chance to talk German again. He was a superb dancer. I had a motor bike. We started going to the bigger dances and visiting other venues. As soon as we arrived, Helmut would find a partner and take to the floor. He was an expert. My steps were much more hesitant. I did get better, very slowly although I was never as good as Helmut.

It was on a Saturday evening in late May 1955 that we went to a dance in the Assembly Rooms in Framlingham. The dance floor was so much better than the one in the village hall and we were both soon dancing. My partner was small and dark and attractive and we danced every dance together. I had met Monica, the girl who was to change my life for ever.

Epilogue

Life became hectic now, what with going to dances, visiting Monica's home and meeting her relatives. All of Suffolk seemed to be related to her. She more than made up for my very few, widely scattered relatives, on my father's side in Canada and on Mother's in Ireland, Australia and New Zealand, with only four aunts in England. Two of these aunts in fact were great aunts called Til and Lil, real Victorian maiden aunts running a boarding house for bachelor gentlemen in Birkenhead. Til was the boss and fawned over her men while Lil was the slave and yet the greater character of the two. She had been a very good tennis player and pianist. Amongst her treasures was a waltz she composed in honour of a Boer War hero, General Sir R Buller, and had published in Liverpool. She lived to be 102.

But now I was in a totally new area of relationships. We would visit this aunt of Monica's or this or that cousin. They mostly lived in farms, some in big rambling houses down long drives - places I had seen from roads but which had always seemed devoid of people.

Another change to the old order of my life came when Mother announced she was going to live in Italy now that I 'was settling down'. On the 6th September 1955, Monica came to Holly Cottage in Marlesford, and this was her first, and for some time her last, meeting with Mother. Here Molly and Richard, Mother's old friends and war-time compatriots, also met Monica for the first time! It was a sort of farewell party for Mother, as she was leaving for Italy on the 14th September. Why was she going? Ostensibly to do some serious writing in a small flat a friend had found for her on Ischia near the island of Capri off Naples. Since her first three novels had been published from 1948 onwards, Mother had only been writing short stories and newspaper articles. She told us she needed peace and atmosphere and sun to be creative. But we were soon to find out that a German writer and thinker had become her soulmate. This was to go on for several years, a great heartache to us.

On August Bank Holiday Monday, Monica and I went to the

Aldeburgh Carnival, joined by Helmut and his girlfriend, and Monica's friend Greta who had been snapped up by Werner, another German over here. His friend Michael Wheeler had asked us all to come along after the carnival to his cottage, Sibton Lodge. What an ideal romantic place. Log fire, only candle light. Werner and Michael played the guitar. We drank wine from Spanish shepherds' wineskins, where you squirted wine down your throat through a tube attached to a leather bladder-like vessel. Laughter, singing, dancing, talking - time flew, no one cared. Sometime in the early hours we must have gone, I can't remember when. Unforgettable!

What did Monica think of all this? This was not a question asked then, but came up many years later when reflecting on this great event in both our lives. There was no one thing where Monica could say "Yes, that was it", or "at that moment I knew". I was so different from her many local contacts and friends, but that may have helped. Monica assured me that she had no pre-conceived notions about the 'German connection'. She judged what she saw and felt, not what other people might hint at or be wary of. She had a very open mind about everyone and was glad she had someone she could talk to, discuss with, ask of and analyse with. We both found we looked at things in much the same way. We felt we were meant for each other and there were no doubts.

Another similarity was that we had both been without one of our parents from the age of two onwards, Monica without her mother and I without my father and a lot of the time with Hildegard as substitute for my mother.

So, understandably we were now almost charging helter-skelter to make up for lost time and gain strength from a new found unity and affection.

In the next two weeks I had to get a move on to find digs as Mother was leaving soon. A Woodbridge friend said I could lodge with board at his Mother's in New Street in Woodbridge.

In the meantime our cottage in Marlesford had been sold. A few of the better pieces of furniture were stored on a farm in Marlesford and I moved to Woodbridge soon after Mother left. In fairness to Mother she gave me a good proportion of the proceeds of the sale of Holly Cottage. This, with some of my own savings bought a small cottage in Hacheston for £750. It was very cheap as it needed a lot doing to it and was very basic.

So now I set about getting the cottage into a good state of repair and with some modernisation and a great deal of decoration. We both did this whenever we had spare time and at weekends.

Now at least we had our own home. What an incentive now to make it a cosy, happy home. Out of the living room window you would look over the low meadows towards the River Ore and the railway line now moving sadly towards its last days.

Monica had trained as a nursery/infant teacher. She was now in a lovely, small village school at Campsey Ash. There was the Headmistress's cottage next door, then the steep pitched roof and red brick of the school with its two classrooms, kitchen and cloakrooms. It had outside toilets and the playground was protected by large pine trees surrounded by fruit bushes and semi-wild flowers. A large swing was the only fixed 'play equipment'. For the rest the children used their imagination with stones, logs and the sand that was everywhere. The school cook and other helpers were nearly all aunts or relatives of the children being taught. Everyone helped at the annual fete or for school plays or outings. The villagers all met twice a day to bring or fetch their children who all walked to school. The local vicar, again the Revd Mark Meynell, gave religious instruction as it was a voluntary aided church school. The chairman of the Governors from the 'Big House' gave prizes and reigned with benevolence over his flock. It all worked. County inspectors would occasionally visit and depart quite happily after a nice cup of tea and scones with the Headmistress, reporting presumably that all was well with Campsey Ash. Monica loved flowers, plants and all to do with nature. Her nature table reflected the countryside around. She would look after the younger children and Mrs Chapman, the Headmistress, would put the final polish on the 'seniors' before they apprehensively went to the 'Big School' in Woodbridge or Framlingham. Monica's car would often be full of pictures and collections to enhance the nature table. I would watch with fascination how she put so much love and care into all her work.

Fetes, theatre, cinema, visit even to a London show and invitations to relatives to have a look at Monica's young man! Usually everyone around here was known by someone or had some connection with the area. I was the mystery-man, many thought I was partly German, having been brought up there, and they had to be quickly reassured as to my pure English blood. Anything German was still suspect, understandably so. Even Monica had lost an aunt during a lone German plane's raid over Framlingham one sunny Sunday afternoon in 1940. The V1 and V2 rockets that I had seen going up had brought fear to the people of Suffolk on their way down.

Monica and I had decided that, if at all possible, we wanted to get engaged at Christmas. Early on a Sunday in December I plucked up courage to ask Monica's father if I might marry Monica. I took ages to get to the point with 'Father'. He agreed except to wonder if we were not being too hasty. It now seemed I was gaining a father again. Anyway we all agreed that after a Christmas engagement we should have a late July wedding.

So at Christmas our news was one of the main talking points. After a large dinner at Home Farm the whole 'clan' seemed to meet at Monica's grandparents' for tea. The men in one room drinking whisky and smoking while putting the world of farming to rights, the ladies gathering in the 'front room' to discuss the latest news on births, marriages and deaths. I was in no man's land until the following year when I was entrusted with the key to the whisky cupboard like a eunuch looking after the harem key. Usually I would end up with the ladies where I was less likely to put my foot in it about nitrogen levels, bushel weights and moisture content of grain.

Now we were approaching 1956, the year of the wedding. My work with the local builder, where I had now finished my training and was paid as a carpenter, was under threat. Work was getting short and I could see the firm was going downhill. I looked around and sounded out various job prospects. Luckily in July someone was leaving their job as a carpenter with the Ministry of Works, Ancient Monuments Branch. I applied and eventually was offered the job. This would be very interesting and rewarding work, restoring local monuments. So now there was something else to look forward to, as this job would start mid-July just before the planned wedding. I would be based at Framlingham Castle, very near Hacheston where we were going to live. The early part of my work with Ancient Monuments was mostly on restoration of the Castle. After many years of neglect much needed to be done to make the Castle visitor-friendly and indeed safe!

As July drew to an end I slowly ceased to live in the real world. Events relating to the impending wedding and the family machine seemed to take me over. So many things had to be done, problems I never knew about or even had the slightest idea of, or how to solve them. I just followed where others led or directed me. I knew everyone meant well and wanted it to be perfect, but I felt so muddled and unsure of what I had to do or was going to do. I just wanted to run off with Monica and be happy by ourselves, but was overwhelmed by the whole giant organisation with church service, reception, speeches, saying the right thing, trying to remember who was who in this stream of well wishers. It was all so lovely and romantic but it was almost lost on me in my confusion and bewilderment.

Ken, my old friend from London, was going to be best man. He was staying with me but was at an even greater disadvantage in hardly knowing anybody. Another far greater handicap beset him in that people at the farm all wanted to calm him and so plied him with drinks. He became calm alright but comatose and walking on cloud nine with all the food, drink and happy people. As to organising anything to do with the wedding arrangements, he was now lost to us! In fact he was sent to meet someone and lost himself for a long time. When he was around he was great fun and reassured me whenever he could.

My mother was unable to afford to come all the way from Italy and then to return, so her lifelong friend Iris Warren from London stood in for her and made a very warm and necessary speech, necessary as the Briscoes were so very thin on the ground. By the end of all the ceremonies and the lovely service in the beautiful flint-clad village church of St Mary in Parham, I was calmer and reassured. Then came the photographs. These were taken by Uncle Jim. He lived in Framlingham, knew everyone and treated it all as a big family party rather than an organised photo-call. From the church door, where all the pictures were taken, we looked out on rolling meadows with sheep gazing on all this mad crowd that suddenly converged on their tranquil scene.

Monica had a lovely set of uncles on her Mother's side, big cheerful life-loving men. They borrowed her father's shotgun, threw up their hired hats on top of the marquee and started firing at them! During the celebrations we were constantly introduced to different friends and relatives and I got more and more confused. Ken by now was asleep in some corner. All Monica and I wanted to do was to get changed and go. But we still had to wait and talk to the next sitting of

Our wedding 1956 St Mary's Church, Parham

1957/58 In Miltenberg with Seppl and Hildegard

all the men and their wives who worked on the farm. Happy red faces and endless plates of food disappeared as if by magic. Drink flowed freely and sly asides were made to us to launch us on our wedded bliss!

Then we were off. Best going-away outfits and shining if slightly worn faces, and a Morris Minor that clattered down the yard with old shoes, cans and stones in hub caps. At last we could escape!

After our return from honeymoon my new job at the castle really got going. First we rebuilt all the wood bridges along the curtain-wall, then a major rebuilding of the main hall and custodian's house roof was started. Beams that had been in place for 400-500 years had been eaten away in many places by death watch beetle. Once the roof was done, 11,000 tiles had to be hung with oak pegs (hand made!) onto their battens.

While we were finishing this job, contractors were laying a main drain along the drive to the castle. Near the Castle Inn they started to unearth human bones, more and more of them. Everything was kept for investigation. Experts from Cambridge came to study and to cata-logue all the remains found. Bone parts of more than 100 humans were found, in all probability Christian Saxons who had been buried near the original wooden castle that was thought to have been built near the present Castle Inn. The bones were taken to Cambridge, examined and returned to Framlingham. I had to make a large oak coffin for them. We loaded this strange cargo on a bier and, after a short service taken by the Rector, the Saxons were re-interred in the churchyard.

Other monuments that came under our care were Orford Castle, Leiston Abbey ruins, Lindsey Chapel (near Hadleigh) and Saxtead Mill, the latter taking over 2 years to rebuild down to the round-house. With the invaluable help of a millwright who came specially out of retirement to advise on the complex structure, we rebuilt the mill, making and jointing all the various parts as would have been done those many years ago. The main oak post cross-beam came from the Tower of London and had 2-foot long tenons on each end to support the whole rotating part of the windmill.

After the hectic activity of 1956, 1957 was a year of taking stock and looking at a new, more meaningful direction for both my life and our new life together. My work in building no longer satisfied me. Church had assumed a new meaning and having my first insight into teaching through Monica, a choice required to be made.

It had to be teaching. But how? Checks were made, contacts consulted and gradually the requirements for teacher training became clear. As a mature (!) student I would need a minimum of 5 'O' level passes.

The irony of it! I, who had always been the despair of teachers, was now hoping to join their ranks.

I settled on a correspondence course. I needed and wanted something now and badly. In 6 months I was there with all the support I could get from Monica. When the results came out I had my 5 'O' levels with an average mark of 72%. So now to apply to a college. Through a family contact I was advised to apply to Redland Training College in Bristol.

1960 Redland Teacher Training College, Finals year. Far right with the black jacket is me and to my right Mr Gegg our first class education tutor

I got an interview (mainly because of the odd application details!) and was accepted for the September 1958 2-year course. I loved the learning experience, an empty brain was all too ready to take all it could get. In my last year at college our daughter was born during final school practice at the new Henbury Comprehensive School at Bristol. The college results were published on the 12th of July, my birthday. How proud I was. I had the only diploma of distinction in the year!

I was then contacted by the Headmaster of Henbury Comprehensive School suggesting I apply for a job there. It was a pioneering school with over 2,000 pupils, full of ambitious and enthusiastic teachers. It was an ideal springboard for quickly gaining many years of experience in a short time.

A special bonus was a new German Department with its head, Helen Bird. As a child she and her parents had always spent their summer holidays in Miltenberg and on a photo she found among her parents' albums was a blond boy she used to play with, probably me! Now our son, Robert, also joined the family.

Suddenly a friend in Essex wrote advising me of a good woodwork teacher's job advertised at the Margaret Tabor School (Secondary Modern, later to become Tabor High School) in Braintree, Essex. As we wanted to be nearer to Grandfather and the farm we decided I take the job if I was offered it. At the interview I also offered German and Building Skills and was accepted.

While thinking of Helen and my later discussions and exchanges of thoughts with her, I found it was she who made me realise that not all Germans had been like my family and friends in Miltenberg. For the first time I was made to realise that not all Germans followed Hitler's ideology to the letter or his fanatical anti-Jewish pro-Aryan theories. Helen's father , also in the teaching profession, had been totally anti-Nazi and had instilled humanitarian values of fairness and tolerance into Helen. Further she assured me of many others that had questioned the Führer's ideas and been actively against them. She told of many instances of opposition to the party-line which made my blind acceptance of it all seem that much more stupid and unthinking. But I could honestly say that none of those with whom I came in contact had sown seeds of doubt in me at any time, and I went on believing, accepting the obvious, at times not even following my own conscience. I had always thought that everyone had joined the Hitler Youth, but not Helen - she had been on the outside, supported and encouraged by her parents to keep up these high standards. So that too had been possible while I had just followed the herd. Mind you, for the sake of the family and the shop, it would have not been politic not to join, and I especially had to be seen to be a true German. Gradually, if belatedly, I was now at last taking a look at what had been happening to me and realising the lack of guidance I had had from anyone in my youth. The main criterion had always been: do what is good for business, for the shop and ultimately for us.

Had we known what was going on? I am often asked this and can only say we could have known if we had delved into rumours that were rife and listened to people who had seen certain things but who were not believed or their stories were not followed up. We may get into trouble with the police and the shop will suffer! Questioning what 'they' did was not done nor even advisable, so gradually more and more was accepted and condoned in the name of the Nazi slogan: Total War to gain Total Victory. And so we blundered on for just sheer survival. We, the young and inexperienced, followed blindly, always thinking we knew better than those old doubting Thomases.

But why were all the Nazi Party documents, party flags, badges and medals put into a strong steel box and buried deep in the back garden just before the Americans arrived? My questioning was only answered with: "You never know! They might come in useful one day!"

It was refreshing now to have Helen show me different points of view based on many underground movements that had been active despite terrible dangers in the very widespread and almost all-seeing all-hearing police state of the later war years. Now I could make sense of people, quite ordinary people, in Miltenberg suddenly not being there any more. They had to move, they have gone away, they probably moved to relatives. Then I put it out of my mind.

When the Americans came we were asked what we had done in and before the war. We lied or said what we reckoned would help us most. Everyone was doing it so why not?

Then, coming home to England, I was again confronted with the stark realities of the evil of Hitler's Germany. I had helped to smash up a Jewish church and chased the Rabbi. Was that right? I had believed that all Germany's problems were part of the larger Jewish conspiracy. And still today I am ill-at-ease with the whole Jewish question. I have to force myself not to invest Jews with special evil powers and sinister motives.

Possibly very little help and guidance on the Jewish question was forthcoming from the Catholic Church. I can never remember our Priest helping us or guiding us on liberal lines. But was he protecting his own very vulnerable position? Many priests and monks were suddenly called up. Would it have been they had dared to speak up against the regime? I now wonder.

Back in England, press and radio were daily blaring out more and more lurid and horrendous stories of camps and mass graves being found in the East, in Poland and in the extensive forest regions of the central European plain. Why did I not know about all this - the extermination camps, the railway sidings that ended abruptly and were places of no return, the policy of eradicating Jews or mixed-race peoples, mentally handicapped or deformed people? The murder of people who disagreed or even questioned - why were they destroyed? Why had my 'family' never said anything about this to me? Could all this be true? Could it be the other side's plot to further discredit the Fatherland? Small reminders of conversations overheard within the family during the war did point to some questioning when Seppl or Willi Schwinn were home on leave and talked about gangs of workers in prison-like uniforms mending or making new roads or clearing war-damaged buildings. Who were they? Jews didn't come into the reckoning; they by all accounts had 'with all their money and American connections' left the country before or at least in 1938. No, these prison-workers were deviants or anti-government agitators. These were people who had not listened to 'our Führer' and had paid the price. Again the conversations used to end with: "Unsere Regierung weiß doch am Besten!" ("Our Government knows best!") And so it was that I had never been part of a questioning family and found it all the harder to come face to face with stark realities in post-war England.

Just before and during the war I was convinced that the root of all Germany's misery and its lack of 'Lebensraum' was due to a conspiracy by the Jews to subjugate and dominate the world economy by their own international network. Perhaps also our Catholic teaching may have influenced my simplistic acceptance of Christ's death by the Jews as another sign of the evil of the Jewish nation. I don't know. No one ever made me face up to or think about what I and others were doing in persecuting Jews.

Did we care or think about foreign workers, nothing more than slave labour in all but name? We saw them, they worked silently and sullenly amongst us, lived in awful conditions, but they were not German, they were often of Slav origin and this was the answer to us. We are better by our racial superiority and they therefore are inferior to us. This is what we were told and believed. Why did no parent or priest point out the terrible wrong of this corollary?

So slowly these ideas became our accepted standards that we need not question. Needless to say, when eventually I started to seriously question all these fixed ideologies, great clouds of guilt began to darken my life and atonement had to be made for these mistakes.

Not that poor Papa Sauter helped matters when once or twice he would shout at me in a fit of temper: "If we hadn't taken you on as our child you might have ended up in a camp like a prison". This hurt me a great deal and I can still remember the implied threat.

As to torture of those in our power, I never saw any, other than the Kristalnacht episode with the poor Jewess and the following day the stoning of the Rabbi. I was 8 at the time and the senior Hitler Youth and party faithful were leading the way.

The influence of my Mother's pro-German friends on my return to England delayed my facing the horror of all that had gone on. Much later in my life, films like 'Schindler's List' still disturbed me a great deal. A visit to Warsaw in the mid nineteen-nineties with a group of farmers and a very fair English guide married to a Polish wife brought home to me the enormity of the obliteration of all that was Jewish and non-Aryan.

Another question then posed itself: How did my real, if new mother fit in with all this? In post-war London an ex-offender against the state had little sympathy from the system. Just coping with rationing, housing shortages and a strange, homesick adolescent mixed-up boy was almost beyond her. She tried hard but had little support from me who blamed all my ills on her. Why didn't she leave me in Germany? My lack of English did not help our relationship. Her best friends, Mollie and Richard, only confused the issue by being anti-government and still very right wing, the forerunners of the National Front. I did listen to them only because I wanted someone to sort out all the muddles in my own mind but it would be a long time before this could and did happen.

Gradually Mother and I did develop a friendship and a sense of loyalty to each other, even if it was just to make some headway and progress in this post-war muddled England. After National Service I had regular work and some sort of future prospects started to emerge. Mother obviously felt I was now more self-sufficient and yet also useful to her in providing a home, repairing and paying for its running and looking after any garden. A relationship that fulfilled our joint needs but had few deeper ties.

Once Mother started to save some money and receiving a small legacy when her father died, she thought of spreading her wings and revisiting Europe, her main love.

When I met Monica and Mother could see that I might soon be making moves to 'fly the nest' she made her move to leave for Italy to work on her writing - and in pursuance of a romantic attachment she wanted to cultivate with a German intellectual, still a restless widow!

This Italian adventure was to last nearly 5 years. Mother would return for good to England soon after Catherine was born in 1960.

To come back to my job change to Essex. I spent a long weekend in Essex looking for a small house or cottage. Eventually a likely cottage came on the scene. Of course it had to belong to a German! A large redheaded lady, breast feeding a baby during the house viewing - which did hinder concentration - extolled the virtues of the cottage especially as Fritz, Siegfried, Gisela, Ingeborg, Günter, Brunhilde and George had all been born here. ('Fertility Cottage' promptly sprang to mind as a house name.) It was obvious they needed more room as the baby's bed was in a drawer in the airing cupboard!

It was a lovely oak-beamed partly weather-boarded Essex cottage. Its large wild garden left plenty of room for expansion. Much renovation and extension work was required, but could all be done gradually by me as and when I had time and the funds.

So with plenty of ideas for our new home and my new school I returned to Bristol and Henbury School, where the seeds of enthusiastic teaching and dedicated work had been sown, nurtured and fertilised.

Monica had to get our move organised while I had but little time to sort out and make a tidy break two-thirds through a school year. We had been very fond of Bristol and had made many friends. My mother too had enjoyed all the arts and amenities of this thriving city. She was to miss them very much.

So Easter came and our meagre belongings were moved to Walnut Tree Cottage, Duck End Green, Rayne near Braintree. The children were much happier. They were not hemmed in by a town but now lived on a green with a few cottages and plenty of space and some other children. Father-in-law found a caravan which was brought from Suffolk to Rayne where Mother could now live in peace in our garden. Her bike gave her freedom to roam this pleasant and flat part of Essex. After Henbury my new, smaller school seemed so much more straightforward, though as yet I had no idea that this would be the school where twelve of my busiest and most fulfilling years would be spent. I had been awarded a graded post and had my very own workshop. Now I could develop my own ideas and my college-inspired work.

This growing Secondary Modern School also drew many children from the outlying villages. The Headmaster wanted to break up a large impersonal school system by having a strong Year Tutor team. Each year had its own Year Tutor who followed right through the whole school-life giving continuity and a strong personal point of contact. I was appointed as one of the first Year Tutors. Then I was asked to supervise up to 200 boys in the school's flourishing Duke of Edinburgh's Award scheme. When a group of boys were awarded their Gold Award I was invited to go with them to Buckingham Palace. I smiled to myself when I was presented to the Duke. Little did he know that I had cut my teeth in youth work in Hitler's outfits!

Later when the school-leaving age was raised I developed a building course (brickwork, carpentry, painting and decorating) to provide practical work for a group of disaffected boys who felt cheated for a further year from going out in the world of work.

I was now on a Scale III salary but had less and less time for my family and myself. How was this state of affairs ever going to change?

This question that I asked myself implied dissatisfaction. Far from it. My arrival in despair, confusion and sadness in those miserable days in Croydon just after the war, the days when I was referred to as 'England's last 'ope' now seemed far away and I had become accepted. My own problems were now shrinking into insignificance while helping others and enjoying acceptance.

I was no longer an outsider of an adoptive family. I now had my very own family as well as my wife's very wide circle of relatives in a rural, stable environment. At long last I, like the trees on the farm, was putting down roots and feeling more secure.

Casually one day when we were visiting Monica's father at Home Farm with his grandchildren, he asked me out of the blue if I would be his executor should anything ever happen to him. To others that may seem at best a nuisance or at worst a thankless task. To me however it was an honour, a vote of confidence that I had never had from anyone. I have never forgotten this and always see all I do for the family farm as a steward of father-in-law's trust in me. I love the farm and its land and buildings, not for their value to me or my family, but

Monica, Paul, Catherine and Robert on holiday in 1973 in Devon

something that I hope will go on for ever and be improved and nurtured by future generations.

And then unexpectedly this office which father entrusted to me became a reality when suddenly he died of a serious heart condition. A local auctioneer and estate agent and myself were executors to his estate. The whole question of the farm's future in Suffolk had to be quickly sorted out. Family conferences and solicitor's advice suddenly replaced the daily school routine. Should the farm be sold or should it be kept going? A cousin of Monica's, Herman Seggons, was willing to manage the farm for a trial period. Monica's brother-in-law, Alfred, was already working on the farm and responsible for all the livestock. Will Paul do the legal and administrative work and look after the building side of the farm? If the answer was yes, then I had to move to the farm and have a simpler teaching job closer to the farm. Would I do it? I felt I had to and went back to my headmaster, Mr White, to present my case. He would be sorry to lose me but he felt the family farm and many people's livelihood had to come first. So with a heavy heart I had to give three months' notice to end my work at Tabor High School at the end of the autumn term. Robert our son was to stay with his aunt in Suffolk from September to start a full school year in his new school in Woodbridge while Monica would stay with Catherine in Essex for her to finish her 'O' level examinations in the following June.

One great fortune in all this was that a job I found in a Woodbridge school, Farlingaye High, involved starting up a new Woodwork Course where the subject had been without a teacher for some time. Of course it was a much simpler job with a very light timetable and a consequent drop in salary. But I needed more freedom to sort out the farm's business and administration that hitherto had been mostly in father-in-law's head and on the back of endless brown used envelopes. Office work was not his first love!

So now a new direction again. It was yet another challenge but one that was made easier by help given from many sides. As the farm's workload dropped, so school work grew over the next 12 years. Gradually a lot of local community work and church work added itself to my

1989 Oak Farm restored barn after 1987 storms

timetable and when in 1988 this area of Suffolk closed Middle Schools, several senior teachers were suddenly offered early retirement. So now at 58 I left Farlingaye High School together with the Head, his deputy and other senior teachers, and in fact my time became more than filled by farm and local work.

Now there was time to look back and make sense of all the ups and downs, the beautiful moments of childhood adventures. Then of dramatic turmoil and brushes with death and destruction, evil and agony. Then the long and tortuous readjustment in an alien land so totally opposed to my adoptive 'fatherland', its ideals, methods and feelings. The sudden jolt of national service back in a now 'occupied' land. This was followed by my life at one of its lowest depths. Then suddenly a much calmer life of tranquil fields, meadows, woods and the quaint villages of Suffolk. A slow healing by time and other influences also engulfed in an area of country life with roots and security. A life less based on material values, but rather on faith in weather, seasons and natural changes that gave comfort and hope.

And yet it also made me value my early experiences, the excitements and dramas that at times dogged my life and at others made it that much more colourful and ultimately meaningful. In all the evil and hate of this era that I lived through I had always found kind people that cared for me when they did not need to. I was loved and helped by people who collectively were branded evil..

It is to all those who added to my quality of life that my thanks go out and I am only sorry that I had to hurt some in the process.

Many would think it an unhappy life, but most of the time we were all so busy coping, and everything moved at such a pace that excitement rather than fear or pain were the hallmark of the war years. Another factor was the unity and bond that held us together and supported us through all those dark days.

The return to loneliness in an alien country was far worse, but again I never had time to lose heart. I just had to fight to keep my head above water until at last I managed to make more sense of my existence. Slowly I started progress into more happy, calmer, open waters. Now I had my own family and with roots firmly put down in Suffolk.

I have talked of the calmer waters of Suffolk and yet my birthplace was London and to that vast city I returned after the war, but the contact with Suffolk, first at Lodge Farm on the Suffolk/Norfolk border, then in East Suffolk around Framlingham, all came about through my Mother's endeavours. In this whole story she has never been a central figure but a very important shaper of my fate. She carried with her her own difficult family background as part of a large late-Victorian family where she, as a rebel, wanted to break into a man's world as a journalist and writer. She chased after rainbows and was impetuous but, with her Irish background, loved a laugh and a good story. Here she was a very good stimulant and fun. She too came to love Suffolk and its people after her often sad or misguided exploits. Right up to the age of 80 she would cycle along the leafy lanes of this county, usually getting lost but always finding home again. She lived with us for most of her last 30 years until her death at the age of 96.

So it was my mother I have to thank for my contact with Suffolk. Here I found a very beautiful rural world. Old villages and monuments to past historic glories. Here I found myself back in the fold of the Church, of community and public work, and working with the farm, its woods and buildings. Here were ponds, and deer, birds and wildflowers in profusion, wide open skies that solved and yet did not make problems. Its people accepted me and trusted me.

With this safe haven and strength I can visit Germany, my other home, and I can come to terms with recurring guilt but one that has no rancour.

Coppicing Historic Queen Mary Wood Oak Farm. 1995/96. Me with 'Gear' and brother in law Alfred with his dog Ben.

Foster Fatherland

Table of historical dates 1933-1945

1933

30 Jan   *Hitler is voted into power as Reich Chancellor*
27 Feb   *The German Parliament building in Berlin is set on fire leading to many arrests*
5 Mar   *In German elections to the Reichstag the NSDAP (Nazi Party) has a majority.*
13 Mar   *Dr Goebbels elected Minister of Propoganda & Population information.*
21 Mar   *In Dachau and near Berlin the first concentration camps are opened.*
10 May   *Public book burning of anti state literature starts.*

1934

4 Sept   *First large scale party rally is held in Nurnberg. Workers holiday scheme: Kraft durch Freude (KDF)- Strength Through Joy- starts in this year.*

1935

       Ferdinand Porsche makes the prototype VW car. It is first called the KDF car.
13 Jan   *Saarland votes by 90.5 % to return to Germany.*
15 Sept   *A citizen's charter is declared by Hitler in Nurnberg aimed at protecting Germany's blood and honour, not recognised by international leaders, but its ultimate aim is the destruction of Jews.*
3 Oct   *Italy invades Abyssinia.*
       National Service re-introduced in Germany.

1936

       The first VW People's car comes off the production line. However, few are ever delivered, with 55,000 going to the army.
7 Mar   *German troops enter the Rhineland.*
26 Mar   *Jewish organisations arrange for 25,000 to flee to Palestine.*
29 Mar   *In a single national party election in Germany the Nazi party gain 99 % of the vote.*
5 May   *The victorious Italian army enters Addis Ababa. The war thus ends.*
1 Aug   *The Summer Olympics are opened in Berlin.*
1 Oct   *Franco becomes Head of State in Spain. The civil war now continues until 1939 with a fascist victory.*
       In the second half of this year Hitler signs a pact with Japan against communism and also:
25 Oct   *A pact with Mussolini to form the Rome- Berlin Axis.*

1937

5 Nov   *War plans made by Hitler to solve the (lack of living space) Lebensraum.*

1938

12 Mar *Austria's Anschluss (joining) with Germany by a vote of 99.75 % (!).*
10 Apr   *Germans are settled in Czechoslovakia, now to be called the Protectorate of Bohmen and Mahren (Bohemia and Moravia).*
9 Nov   *Kristallnacht sanctioned by Goebbels.*

1939

15 Mar *German troops march into Czechoslovakia.*
25 Mar *France and England pledge to help each other in case of attack.*
25 Mar *From now on membership of the Hitler Youth is compulsory from 10-18.*
28 Mar *Spanish civil war ends with victory for Franco.*
31 Mar *England guarantees help to Poland in case of attack by Germany.*
7 Apr *Italian troops march into Albania.*
28 Apr *The Polish government receives a note from Germany cancelling the non-aggression pact of 1934.*
19 May *Poland and France sign a secret military pact.*
15 July *The first reservists are called up in Great Britain.*
30 Aug *General mobilisation in Poland.*
1 Sept *World War II starts with the bombardment of Danzig and the invasion of Poland by German troops.*
3 Sept *France and Great Britain declare war on Germany.*
4 Sept *600,000 people, mostly children and older people, are evacuated from London.*
17 Sept *Russian forces occupy eastern Poland.*
25 Sept *A big air strike is launched by Germany against Warsaw.*
2 Oct *21 American States confirm neutrality*
4 Nov *Through President Roosevelt the neutrality policy of America is relaxed.*
16 Nov *Australia declares general conscription for all men over 21.*
30 Nov *Russia attacks Finland and is excluded from the League of Nations on 14 Dec.*
23 Dec *The IRA storm an ammunition depot in Dublin.*

1940

9 Apr *The neutral countries of Denmark and Norway are attacked by Germany.*
10 May *The offensives against neutral Belgium, Luxembourg and Netherlands begin.*
10 May *Winston Churchill takes over as Prime Minister from the dismissed Neville Chamberlain.*
11 May *General mobilisation of Swiss Army.*
2 June *The people of Britain are urged to hand in old iron.*
10 June *After evacuation of allied troops, Norway capitulates.*
10 June *Italy attacks France and joins Germany in the war.*
14 June *German troops occupy Paris*
14 June *The first prisoners are interned in Auschwitz.*
15 June *Soviet troops occupy three baltic states.*
17 June *Marshall Petain forms a government in France.*
18 June *Charles de Gaulle forms the Free French National Committee in London.*
21 June *Britain recognises the Polish government in exile.*
22 June *A cease fire is declared in vanquished France by Germany.*
3 July *After repeated refusals to join the British, the fleet of the Vichy Government is destroyed at Oran in Algerian waters by British Warships.*
18 July *Following Japanese pressure Great Britain has to block the main supply route of the Chinese Government.*
13 Aug *The Battle of Britain begins.*
21 Aug *Trotsky is murdered by Soviet agents while in exile in Mexico.*
20 Sept *French food rationing is stepped up to provide Germany with more food.*
27 Sept *Germany, Italy and Japan sign a three power pact against the USA.*
14 Nov *The centre of Coventry is heavily damaged by German bombing.*
15 Nov *The main ghetto to intern 400,000 people is built in Warsaw.*

22 Nov   Ireland reinforces its neutral status.
9 Dec   A successful offensive is mounted against Italian positions in North Africa.
17 Dec   Lease Lend agreements are outlined by President Roosevelt.

1941

14 Feb   German troops arrive in North Africa to help Italy.
4 Mar   British troops land in Greece to protect it against German attack.
6 Apr   German troops attack Greece and Jugoslavia.
10 May   Hess, Hitler's deputy, parachutes into Britain, near Glasgow.
12 May   The first programmed computing machine is launched by Konrad Zuse called "Zuse Z.3"
20 May   German paratroops land on Crete.
22 June Without declaring war Germany invades Russia on a wide front.
30 July America negotiates with Russia for the supply of weapons.
         late Aug Lale Anderson's song "Lili Marlene" has it's first broadcast.
25 Aug   Soviet and British troops occupy neutral Iran to secure oil wells.
11 Sept US President Franklin Delano Roosevelt orders that German and Italian ships that
         stray into United States waters are to be fired on.
5 Dec   The German offensive on Moscow is repulsed by a counter attack of the Red Army.
7 Dec   The Japanese attack on Pearl Harbor brings America into the war.
11 Dec   Hitler declares that Germany is at war with America.

1942

1 Jan   The United Nations Charter is born
16 Jan   Japanese troops enter Burma
20 Jan   The 'final solution' of the Jewish question is discussed in Germany by all main party
         members. A map showing the number of Jews in various parts of Europe gives a total of
         16,618,868 living in German and occupied territories.
21 Jan   German General Rommel starts a counter offensive in Libya.
15 Feb   Singapore capitulates to the Japanese.
28 Mar   The first carpet bombing attack by the RAF destroys most of Lubeck town centre.
30 May   The first 1,000 + RAF bomber attack destroys the whole of central Cologne in a matter
         of 90 minutes.
2 Nov   In North Africa the German- Italian forces evacuate El Alamein.
11 Nov   Southern France is occupied by German troops.
22 Nov   The Stalingrad trap is closed on the 6th German Army.

1943

27 Jan   Daytime raids by American aircraft begin.
30 Jan   First radar controlled bombing by RAF on Hamburg.
31 Jan   The 6th Southern Germany Army Group capitulates in Stalingrad and the Northern
         group follows on 2 February. The battle of Stalingrad is over.
18 Feb   Goebbels announces "Total War"
30 Apr   The Bergen-Belsen concentration camp is opened.
13 May   The German-Italian Africa Army capitulates.
17 May   The British "bouncing" bomb destroys the Mohne and Eder dams in north west
         Germany.
24 May   Because of high losses the U-Boat offensive against allied shipping is suspended.
5 July   The last German offensive in Russia starts in the southern Kursk sector.
10 July Allied troops land in Sicily.
25 July Mussolini is arrested by the King of Italy.

13 Aug The first allied bombing raid on parts of Vienna.
3 Sept The allied invasion of Europe's mainland is started in southern Italy.
12 Sept Mussolini is freed from his mountain prison by German paras.
13 Oct The new Italy declares war on Germany.

1944

19 Jan The last German air offensive against English towns begins.
22 Jan Another landing on the beaches of Italy at Anzio.
1 Mar   The German labour minister Fritz Saukel puts the number of forced labourers in Germany at 7 million.
4 June Rome is occupied by allied troops.
6 June Allied invasion begins on the beaches of Normandy.
12 June The first V.1 rocket is fired on England.
14 June Half a million volunteers from abroad are now in the armed German SS.
20 June USA ships destroy the Japanese carrier fleet near the Phillipines.
22 June The Red Army mounts its greatest offensive which leads to the collapse of the central German Army Group.
15 July Rommel, the former North Africa army commander and now leading the army group B in France, challenges Hitler to end the war.
20 July Hitler survives the attempt on his life by Count Stauffenberg. The Count is executed that evening.
5 Aug   Ann Frank and family are arrested in Amsterdam. She is to die just before the end of the war, age 15.
25 Aug Paris is liberated.
8 Sept The first V.2 rocket is launched against London.
12 Sept Tito becomes sole leader of the Jugoslav resistance.
20 Oct Jugoslavia and Russian troops free Belgrade.
21 Oct Aachen becomes the first German city to be occupied by the Allies.
16 Dec Hitler orders the start of the last ditch Ardennes offensive.
17 Dec Training begins in America of bomber pilots who are to drop the atom bombs.

1945

12 Jan The Russian winter offensive starts.
27 Jan The Soviet army liberates the Auschwitz extermination camp.
30 Jan Hitler's 12th anniversary in power when he swears to the final victory.
11 Feb End of Yalta conference.
14 Feb Several heavy air raids on Dresden cause great damage.
24 Mar British troops cross the Rhine at Wesel.
12 Apr Harry Truman succeeds Roosevelt as President following the latters sudden death.
17 Apr 325,000 German soldiers lay down their arms following total encirclement in the Ruhr area.
25 Apr US and Russian troops meet each other on the river Elbe.
28 Apr Mussolini is summarily executed by partisans.
28 Apr Hitler elects Admiral Donitz and J Goebbels as his successors.
29 Apr German troops lay down their arms in Italy.
30 Apr Hitler commits suicide, together with all his family in Berlin. Donitz becomes President of Germany.
7 May   In Reims a German delegation signs an unconditional surrender.

The war in Europe is over.

5 June *The four allied powers take over Germany and confirm the 4 military zones; American,*
British, French and Russian.
6 Aug *The first atom bomb is dropped on Hiroshima.*
2 Sept *Japan surrenders.*

World War II is at an end.